DUBAI HIGH

DUBAI HIGH

A Culture Trip

MICHAEL SCHINDHELM

with photographs by
AURORE BELKIN

Arabian Publishing

Dubai High: A Culture Trip

© Michael Schindhelm 2011
Photographs © Aurore Belkin 2011

First published in 2011 by Arabian Publishing Ltd
4 Bloomsbury Place, London WC1A 2QA
Email: arabian.publishing@arabia.uk.com

Edited by Sharon Sharpe
from a translation by Amy Patton of the original German edition,
Dubai Speed: Eine Erfahrung
München: Deutscher Taschenbuch Verlag, 2009

A catalogue card for this book is available from the British Library

ISBN: 978-0-9558894-7-9

Typesetting and digital artwork by Jamie Crocker, Artista-Design, UK
Printed and bound by Berforts, Stevenage, UK

CONTENTS

Preface	7
January	9
February	58
March	69
April	93
May	130
June	152
July	167
August	194
September	206
October	219
November	222
December	232

PREFACE

I lived and worked in Dubai from 2007 to 2009. This journal of 2008 condenses my experiences there, and focuses on the issue of public culture, just one aspect of this extraordinary city's dizzying rise and its journey into an uncertain future. Some characters and episodes have been fictionalized in deference to political sensitivities and to the privacy of various individuals. The diary is none the less an authentic and accurate account of the substance of my experiences.

Two years on, the future of Dubai and its people remains in the balance. Even so, I am convinced that the Gulf States, despite their much publicized paradoxes, inequalities and lack of accountability, offer some hope for a political and social alternative to the unrest, social injustice and religious fanaticism of some of their neighbours. Success will depend on genuinely open dialogue – a conversation that has perhaps only just begun.

Michael Schindhelm

I

1 January

From the sea, even a desert offers the promise of solid ground beneath the feet – a firm landfall that beckons across the water to those voyaging from afar. But from the air, this piece of desert is a monstrous, glittering lizard that seems to writhe in the darkness.

The plane banks over a sprinkling of ships' lanterns. It takes a second glance to realize that the coastal lights are strung not just horizontally but also thrust upwards into the blackness, the illuminations of a vertical city soaring in that transitional zone where desert and Gulf merge. Sporadic fireworks burst in the heavens as if in celebration of our arrival – evanescent sparkles swallowed by the night. A background murmur rises from the crew as they move from row to row quietly issuing their instructions. Below us now, the ground is divided into rectangular plots with cranes and construction vehicles blinking into life, even at this unseemly hour. This time last year I was frantically calling around to find a replacement witch for the afternoon performance of *Hansel and Gretel*.

Immediately on landing I pull my phone from my pocket, annoyed with myself but unable to resist switching it on. It's one o'clock in the morning, Central European Time: New Year's Day. Perhaps someone close has spared me a thought and sent a friendly text to mark the occasion. But there's just a message from a journalist, sent during a stopover in Zurich seven hours ago. The man knows I am on my way here, and why. That's what I get for shooting my mouth off to various acquaintances and former colleagues in recent weeks. Tomorrow morning, I expect, in some neon-lit office smelling of overheated computers, bitter coffee and lemon-scented floor cleaner, he'll cobble together a story of sorts from the bits and pieces he's gleaned. I'm at once curious to know if the piece will be favourable, and virtuously aware that it's foolish to be concerned by such things. A new world beckons.

The immediate priority to get a fix on my bearings comes as a welcome distraction. I'm caught up in hordes of passengers converging from all directions from other aircraft, like so many colourful, jostling herds of livestock off to market. There's a buzz in the air and excitement radiates from the faces around me. Maybe it's the thrill of the unknown, or perhaps it's the celebrations – impossible to say whether it's the place or the occasion.

A few hundred metres on and my mobile trills with text salvos from the state telecom company Etisalat enticing me on desert safaris, hot-air-balloon trips, a visit to the gold souk. On my way to the immigration counter I'm assailed by a group of middle-aged Brits draped in tinsel and wearing paper hats, arms linked in a boozy rendition of *Auld Lang Syne*. There are always those who know how to enjoy themselves. As often as not, it's the British.

There are four counters issuing work permits: one each for Arab, Asian and African immigrants and one for Europeans and Americans, the latter unmanned. A crush of bodies besieges the others: immigrant workers from India, Bangladesh and Pakistan. A young Emirati waves me over from behind the African counter and I wait in line behind two tall lads with Tanzanian passports who look to be in their early twenties at most. One of them twirls a string of pearl prayer beads and now and then flashes me a flawless African smile. The Emirati official sports a swan-white *dishdash* and has a slim, handsome face framed by a close-trimmed beard. I watch with nervous anticipation as he straightens the already perfect *ghutra* on his head before thumping a stamp on the document in front of him. Once the Tanzanians have been waved through, he inspects my passport and mutters the German salutation, "*Grüß Gott!*" I want to ask him where he acquired that one, but already he's handed back my passport with a double-page document glued inside.

According to the scant information sent with a copy of my work contract, after clearing customs I am to be met by someone brandishing a sign with my name on it. But all I see is another jostling multitude pressed against the barrier, calling out in English and Arabic, Hindi and Bulgarian, Urdu and Chinese. The only familiar face gazes down from a poster: a tennis player posing next to a coffee machine. And then the heat overpowers me, and the humidity, but I feel strangely and suddenly uplifted by the chaos, by the whoops and screeches of meeting and greeting. I scan the crowd and spot a person, possibly Indian, observing the mêlée with professional boredom. I wonder whether he might be my man. He fans himself, insouciant and seemingly indifferent to the fact it's now 4.30 a.m. and there's a four-row, eighty-metre-long queue ahead for the taxi stand. He pauses long enough for me to see that his "fan" is actually a name board, the combination of letters resembling something an Urdu-speaking Indian from Thiruvananthrapuram might write if he were asked to spell my name. I venture a smile. He accepts my handshake with the customary Indian head wobble, gestures me aside and manoeuvres my luggage trolley through the crowds and on to the car park. His minivan feels like a freezer inside and smells of chewing gum. We head out in heavy traffic on the highway through the city, past skyscrapers, billboards and neon advertisements. At some point my head slams into the front seat and we pull into another car park.

It's pitch black, and someone is calling me. Still half asleep I wonder why the voice is so indistinct. It's message is that I'm away from home. In Europe church bells wake you, but not at this hour – "ungodly", to us. I stagger to my feet, push the two heavy curtains aside and peer through the window, but fail to pinpoint any minaret between the lifeless walls. The sound seems omnidirectional and, to

my bleary imagination, to be emanating from the bathroom. This is what I call schizophonia. Am I hallucinating? I crawl back under the blanket; the room is as cold as the minivan a few hours ago. I make a mental note to examine the air conditioning later as the voice outside commands my attention. It stretches the vowels, squeezing them compactly between gums and tongue until all that remains is an extended, finely modulated series of notes. *Prima la musica, dopo le parole* – First the music, and then the words. A phrase that can be applied to more than just opera, clearly.

And then I'm sucked into a memory loop that has cost me many a sleepless night in recent months: the blow-up with the director of Handel's *Israel in Egypt*, who wanted to burn a Qur'an in the last act to point up the religious intolerance of our times. Visions crowd my mind: camera teams from at least twenty countries swarming outside the Berlin opera house as the story took hold; the journalists at the press conference, indignant faces glistening with sweat, as if I'd insulted them personally by opposing the performance; accusations of intellectual cowardice and self-censorship, then my resignation without notice; and the silence that followed. For a few weeks no one seemed to want to talk to me and I retreated to a forest cabin near Clausthal in the Harz mountains, where I roamed the foggy, deserted autumn trails by day and drank enough herb liqueur in the evenings to nod off in front of the television, all the time wrestling with the same burning question: What is a failed opera director, who has trained for little else, supposed to do with the rest of his life?

2 January

The hotel is less glamorous than the one I stayed in on my only previous visit. It was built, I'd say, in the 1980s, and its gloomy corridors are impregnated with the sweat of expatriates from East and West who swarm to this city to try their luck, like the young Indian I pass on my way to breakfast. He's struggling with a vacuum cleaner outside one of the rooms but the moment he senses my presence he stiffens to attention and salutes me with a "Hi, Sir!" He looks tired. His hair is streaked with gel yet he is hardly more than an adolescent.

My employer is a property development outfit belonging to a government-owned holding company. It's one of many in this city. The business model seems to work as follows: each is granted a piece of land by His Highness, the ruler, somewhere between beach and desert, harbour and airport, and in return for its investment is permitted to operate in similar fashion to the "free zones", exempt from taxation and the normal requirement of operating in partnership with a local sponsor. Thanks to an invasion of tourists and foreign companies, there is a voracious demand for housing, hotels, entertainment facilities, offices and infrastructure.

People are drawn here to earn and spend. They come to consume and, in the process, end up themselves being consumed. Lured by the promise of plentiful work and tax-free salaries, most foreign workers and business people stay for a few years at most. Holiday-makers arrive on long-haul stopovers or stay to take advantage of the promotional rates at newly opened resorts where their budget stretches twice as far as it would in the Mediterranean or the Alps. Eight million tourists arrive here every year and stay on average a week. Hardly anyone comes intending to stay indefinitely. Even so, business is booming. My company's projects are calculated in the billions and planned for rapid completion over vast swathes of land. It was launched just a year ago and has already recruited 800 employees from forty-five countries and begun seventeen large-scale projects. With so much money on the table the company's ambitions have outgrown the available Gulf coastline and it is extending its reach to Morocco, Oman, Turkey and Vietnam, constructing offices, hotels, villas and, naturally, shopping malls. Its vaulting ambition is proclaimed by its very name: Al Adheem – The Most Magnificent.

I had expected to get straight down to work but today, of all days, is the company excursion to a multiplex cinema boasting at least seventeen screens. There's a veritable host of hands to shake and people to nod at on my first day. Then comes a face I recognize:

Azad, a fiftyish Iraqi lead consultant with a Santa paunch and an ironic twinkle beneath his bushy eyebrows who, on my first visit, had introduced me to the building development plan for the project I've come to work on. There's no getting to him though, separated as we are by a throng of Russian, Indian and Arab women, some of them veiled and all of them under thirty, handing one another popcorn and Coke.

In the foyer I run into the gaunt Jordanian who, during my contract negotiations, called me in Harz to explain the thinking behind the new cultural centre planned to accommodate the proposed opera house and theatre complex. The heavy specs accentuate his pallor and deadpan expression and I can't help visualizing him with a bushy mullah beard. Perhaps he senses something. With a quizzical eye, he declares that he remembers me as much younger – a touch provoking given that I've just turned forty-six. True, I've aged since my previous visit to Dubai, but only by five weeks. A suitable riposte eludes me as he proffers a hasty handshake and slips into the auditorium.

Following, I find about three hundred people inside waving to one another, laughing and settling into their seats to watch *Man of the Year*, starring Robin Williams. Meanwhile, two of my new colleagues have taken up position in front of the screen and are attempting a PowerPoint presentation with tables and cartoons illustrating news snippets from the company's daily grind. Though they're speaking English, much of what they're saying is lost on me, though I suspect it has something to do with corporate identity and how to foster a good company spirit. Parking spaces are apparently in short supply, some people are switching offices with puzzling frequency, and one woman wearing jeans, a headscarf and dangly earrings the size of beer mats, wants to know why senior management get more holidays than everyone else. A blonde woman in her fifties comes to the front to offer justification. She has a Swedish-sounding name and works, presumably, in the personnel department. Far from being at ease, she prowls before her audience like a caged beast. Someone in the audience demands that one of the executives come forward but no one jumps to the Swede's aid. So she unclips her microphone and takes a seat in the auditorium.

I sit and brood on my brief encounter with Mohammed the Jordanian. He's the one who is to familiarize me with Al Adheem and its prestigious new project and today's event presents the first opportunity. Here, after all, is where the staff are supposed to get to know each other. But he is nowhere to be seen. The lights go down, the opening credits roll and … three-quarters of the audience gets up to leave, as if they had suddenly and simultaneously remembered they'd left their cars in a no-parking zone. I feel pretty superfluous in here. The only difference between this and multiplex cinemas everywhere is that the smell of greasy popcorn is neutralized by the fiercely efficient air conditioning and an ambient temperature of less than 20 degrees. The Man of the Year has yet to be revealed but I can stand the refrigeration no longer.

3 January

My office is in the Emirates Business Tower, supposedly the most prestigious skyscraper in the city. It soars alongside its somewhat shorter twin, the Emirates Hotel, from a prominent position along the corridor of tower blocks flanking a ten-lane highway of slowly creeping 'rush-hour' traffic. After a series of misunderstandings with the Emirati receptionist, I finally run Mohammed to earth on the 4th floor. He still doesn't seem to have time for me and blinks at me dubiously through the heavy black frames of his glasses before leading me to a makeshift, six-square-metre cubbyhole with two bare desks and a telephone. Someone's sitting there already but the woman, in an *abaya* and black headscarf, betrays no sign of expecting me or of being particularly concerned by my arrival. Mohammed disappears. Fatma, it turns out, is Mohammed's secretary and con-descends to fire me curt answers over her shoulder to questions she probably finds intrusive. Determined not to let myself be peeved by anything today, I resign myself happily enough to it all.

During the course of the hours that follow we strike up something approaching a conversation. Fatma came here from California with her husband three years ago. They've since moved to a neighbouring city where apartments are more affordable than the spiralling rents of Dubai. Her day starts at five o'clock in the morning, when the traffic is light, which means she can leave work early before the evening rush hour hits.

Fatma has little to do. Mohammed takes care of everything himself. She reads the Qur'an at length in the morning and again in the afternoon. She never had the time for that in the States. Eventually the ice thaws and she begins to ask me questions. Where am I from? Yes, she says, she's heard of Berlin, but she seems to be under the impression it's somewhere in China. Below us the traffic whirrs by and I spot a motor-racing team – belonging, most likely, to the Sheikh, says Fatma with a shrug. The motorcade glides past a forest of scaffolding and construction cranes silhouetted against the sinking sun and a desert backdrop stretching to the horizon.

Later, I take a peek around outside the cubbyhole and meet a few new colleagues: men and women, in their thirties mainly, from countries as diverse as Iran and Australia, and occupying cubbyholes similar to mine. They belong to the Strategy Department and carry out research on market conditions for tourism projects in various parts of the world. They find it hard to believe their company has hired a cultural director. "A cultural director?" they say, "Really?"

4 January

At around noon today I bought myself a local mobile phone, as I've been bombarded with international calls on my German one. The reason is a DPA (German News Agency) report claiming that I'm an expert on Gulf culture, who is all set to lead projects involving billions in subsidies and in direct competition with ambitious neighbours already in business with the Louvre and other international cultural organizations. It's news to me – the competition and the billions. For the past five weeks my mind has been taken up with more idealistic schemes for this place of unimaginable riches, dreaming up scenarios in which art and artists subvert the lust for dollars and dirhams; in which they put this glut of capital to higher purpose and find the hidden path out of global consumption and into global culture; in which they discover a philosopher's stone that works in reverse and converts the greed for gold into curiosity for the Other.

I keep all this stuff to myself, of course, and my interviews with journalists brief, for reasons of cost as much as anything else – I'm probably paying two-thirds of the phone charges. Where on earth did these people get my mobile number?

They all ask the same question: How is it possible to work for these Sheikhs? They all voice the same objections: oil money, ecological footprint, exploitation of Asian workers, censorship, disenfranchised women, forbidden sexuality, wanton capitalism, crazed consumerism …. One radio station broadcasts me live in the middle of the news and I'm too daft to hang up. I can hear soundbites of a chanting Palestinian crowd in Jerusalem, calling for death to Israelis because there have been more casualties and dead among their own. When I finally come on to do what I'm asked, that is to describe the cultural situation here, the interviewer gives me about thirty seconds before demanding to know when I'll be showing an opera featuring the symbolic burning of the Qur'an. I get no chance to protest. He interrupts to thank me for my contribution as another voice comes on the line with an emergency traffic bulletin.

I casually surf the internet for reactions. The city I have been trying to settle in for the past three days is misspelled in some reports or confused with another up the coast. One commentator even places me in Kuwait. I find I am being judged and the verdict, for the most part, is less than flattering: I am a culture-industry football coach past his prime who is now more concerned with his pension arrangements. Having recently demonstrated my opportunistic attitude to political pressure it is, apparently, little wonder that I come looking for bread in a dictatorship. One wag refers to the German state I was born in, describing me as a Thuringian (a kind of sausage) out of the frying pan, into the fire. Another wonders if I

have finally lost my mind – which is indeed something no one can ever be really certain of.

Bumping into Mohammed in the corridor later, I can't help enquiring about the status of the press release we agreed announcing my appointment. I also want to know when we can begin work on the project itself. For three days I have dutifully come to work at eight every morning, taken my seat in the cubbyhole, studied the strategy papers available to me, discussed with Fatma the relative merits of various sandwich peddlers, and waved at colleagues through the frosted-glass partitions.

Mohammed blinks at me, his habitual air of scepticism supplemented this time by a cocked and distinctly ironic eyebrow. Rather than answer my question he establishes that I have not shaved. I tell him I have sported a five o'clock shadow for years and cast a scrutinizing glance at the shadow under his own chin. "Oh, you'd better watch it there," cautions Mohammed. "Here you either wear a real beard or none at all. Anything else might be taken as insulting."

I have no desire to bandy words about beard lengths with this little fellow ten years my junior and enquire again about the press release. He puts me off, muttering something vague about sometime during the coming week, but assures me I will be able to look over the draft beforehand. His gaze is now fixed on my right shoulder, as if a cockroach had taken up residence there. There will have to be a photo, he announces, a photo in which I am clean-shaven. I counter by reminding him he also has to get me together with the theatre-building project team. And with an absentminded nod Mohammed vanishes over the threshold into his office.

5 January

Here is where it all began, just a hundred metres from my hotel in the heart of old Dubai. The original little town of merchants and pearl divers grew up on either side of the mouth of a saltwater creek that winds its way from the Gulf coast deep into the desert.

Few written records exist, but what there are relate how the fort, now a museum and near my hotel, was built in 1799 when Dubai was a dependent of the settlement of Abu Dhabi. In 1833, members of the Al Maktoum family of the Bani Yas tribe left Abu Dhabi for Dubai and settled here, establishing the dynasty that still rules today.

By the late 19th century it was a thriving commercial port and boomed when the Sheikh of the time abolished taxes and customs duties. He encouraged an influx of Persian traders, gave them land by the Creek and invited them to build and stay. Dubai's current mix of locals and expats was foreshadowed long ago.

Everyone born in Dubai before 1970 – Emirati and foreigner – grew up somewhere around here. Change came in the 1960s with the discovery of oil, which fuelled a building boom. The old town's original residents left the district for finer houses along the beaches of Jumeirah and in new suburbs in the desert. The Asian community – the majority Indian – stayed behind.

The west side of the Creek is known as Bur Dubai, the east side as Deira. Nowadays, Deira is home to secretaries and bookkeepers, porters and taxi drivers, street-food stands and small businesses. Its low-rise buildings, of 1960s and '70s construction, with their neon advertisements for Indian jewellery and textiles, Chinese household goods, and carpets from Turkey, Iran and Azerbaijan, are a reminder of a more recent past when Dubai was no more glitzy than any other Arab city.

Today the Creek teems with *abra*s, the little motorized water taxis that criss-cross the Creek with their passengers sitting back-to-back on bare wooden benches. You can cross from Bur Dubai to Deira for a single dirham. Fifty years ago, before the underpass and bridges were built and before the shallow areas were dredged to allow vessels constant transit, anyone running late in the evening had to wade or swim to the other shore.

This is where the Deira cultural complex is to be erected: on a deserted spot between markets, car parks and an abandoned jetty. Here, where pearl fishers organized their diving expeditions and 19th-century Persian merchants hawked their wares, where tourists now jostle in the canopied souks and where gold and incense is sold alongside Rolexes fake and genuine.

At the ruler's behest, my employer is to spend three years and half a billion US dollars building on about eighty thousand square metres of this wasteland, in such a way that the roof of the building will accommodate three stages and an exhibition hall. The design approved by the Sheikh is by Swedish-Yemeni architect Touitou, who has never worked in the Middle East but makes up for it by being one of the hottest stars on the scene from San Francisco to Hong Kong.

I find Azad's office on a container vessel on the Creek. The room is strewn with glossy brochures for some of his other development projects, an aerial photograph of the Creek hangs on the wall, a Cimbali coffee machine dispenses high-octane espresso, and dominating it all are five padded wingback chairs that might be straight from Starbucks. We could be in an advertising agency but for the rocking of his office when a bigger dhow docks next door.

Azad's only employee is Cecilia, a young Argentinian assigned to him by Al Adheem's Marketing Department, and I suspect she's here to determine how many opera aficionados will be prepared to shell out three or four hundred euros for a *Traviata* with Renée Fleming in September 2013.

Azad has a way of curling his lip as if he has something of profound import to convey, before launching into a joke. He has a fund of anecdotes and the back-stories take several minutes to unfold. We are well into our meeting and have yet to get round to the project in hand as I learn that he moved here four months ago from Norway, where he lived for twenty-five years having fled Iraq during the war with Iran. He's Kurdish and likes to poke fun at his own people. Cecilia doesn't get the jokes. She has a fine-featured face and the horror-struck pallor of someone who's just witnessed a stabbing.

Eventually we get down to the business of blueprints and spatial concepts. Azad leads me to a three-dimensional plastic model overlaid by a shimmering blue membrane. It has a skewed octagonal base with a tapering sculpture extruded from it, like an enormous flame darting from a pyramidal roof. No right angles, everything made to look soft and organic. I suppose I ought to be impressed but all I can think of is a chocolate Easter bunny and the anthroposophists' twee little houses around the Goetheanum in Dornach, Switzerland. The building is to be 120 metres tall at its apex. How, I wonder, is anyone supposed to get three stages and an exhibition hall into this melting chocolate castle?

I observe that size isn't everything, at least not in art. The tallest tenor is not necessarily the one with the most thrilling voice. Azad pulls me aside when I start to rant about it being impossible to perform classical opera in a room with 3,000 seats. He can see how that might be true, he says in a conciliatory tone, but our employers didn't call themselves 'The Most Magnificent' for nothing. The time will come when I can express my misgivings in the appropriate place.

For now, he thinks it better not to question the number of seats.

Cecilia helps Azad spread the architects' drawings and photographs on the table. I find myself zoning out on the caffeine, the intermittent hum of the inefficient air-conditioning unit, the rocking motion of the boat and the noise outside. Sitting barely above the waterline, we are drowned out by the raucous voices of merchants loading their wares from the wharf: baby food from Bulgaria and ceramic plates from Cyprus.

Suddenly the architect's drawings morph before my eyes into a three-dimensional, walk-in animation of the Easter bunny. I'm stepping inside, shuffling over the pale blue marble foyer as if I had felt slippers on my feet and Azad is leading me to the box office. I have to throw my head right back to gauge the giddy height of the ceiling. "The ruler's youngest wife would like a little museum on the left hand side," Azad murmurs; as to what for, he's sure I'll come up with something. Then his friendly baritone lures me towards the main stage. We glide past VIP lounges upholstered in red and yellow velvet and hung with gold-framed mirrors in which I can see no reflection. Then we're plunged in darkness. We must be standing in an unlit area backstage. Something dangles from the fly tower above. I can't make it out, but it seems to be a pair of high-heeled shoes. I hear Azad telling me to stay where I am until the light comes on. But the light doesn't come on and Azad has quit talking. I imagine I must be standing directly in front of the orchestra pit. There's a cool, slightly musty draft coming from down there. Decay, I think, though not even built yet. Now I see Azad's face, alarmingly close to mine, with Cecilia's beside it. Their lips are moving but I hear nothing.

Outside on the wharf someone heaves me into an armchair and I recover at once. The salty air is greasy with heat and exhaust fumes from the engines of the *abra*s but it feels good to me. I attribute the incident to a lack of sleep over the past few nights. I have been waking consistently at daybreak, stirred by the wailing of the muezzin and my own apprehension about the ordeals I might need to brace myself for in the day ahead. "Welcome back," says Azad. Cecilia hands me a glass of water and I manage to talk her out of calling a doctor. I passed out for at least two minutes, it seems. And in that time I took a virtual tour of the building, I tell them, arranging my features in what I hope is a comical expression.

They are not easily persuaded and insist on accompanying me back to my hotel. I flatly refuse. There is no shaking off Azad though, who tags along as I thread my way back onto the street through stacked crates, cardboard boxes and bales of fabric.

For a moment, I think I'm experiencing an auditory hallucination when I hear Azad humming something from *The Magic Flute.* Then he jumps up on a box and imitates Papageno's aria in a thin and wavering falsetto. He bobs at the knees and, screwing his eyes up with a grin, points a thumb over his shoulder to two young women in white headscarves waiting by the roadside for a taxi. He mimes bundling them into one of the wooden crates lying about – the ones traders use to transport goats. I fear Azad may be one of those irrepressible jokers unable to get through the day without a public audience, but no one in this clamour of loading and unloading seems to take the slightest notice. The shrouded women step into a taxi and my Iraqi Papageno hops off the box. "Did you recognize the music?" he asks, fumbling for his sunglasses in his shirt pocket and indicating with a nod that I should follow him. I'm dazzled by the setting sun. Noticing my hesitancy, he leads me gently by the arm.

Azad chats about the 1980s when he came to Dubai to work for a property development company for the first time. In those days the Arabs were no more competent at running their businesses than they are now, he insists. He glances round and drops his voice to a conspiratorial tone: "The British never managed to teach these people efficiency. They would have been better off with the Germans." Azad's father was a university professor in Baghdad at one time and admired German culture above all others. So much so, he had his son learn the language. "If it weren't for that complete idiot," says Azad, meaning Hitler, "the world would be speaking German today."

We amble along in silence for a while. Seagulls skim the Creek and the ripples shimmer in the dying light of the sun. The pinnacles of the skyscrapers on Sheikh Zayed Road nudge the sky beyond Bur Dubai. A landscaped car park, deserted but for a hillock of artificial palm trees, fades into the dusk. Vehicles on the Maktoum Bridge switch on their lights.

"Mohammed is an imbecile," snarls Azad, the colour draining from his face. "You wouldn't believe how some people in this part of the world regard Kurds. He's one of those snotty-nosed kids who, from the very first handshake, makes it perfectly clear he looks on you as subhuman, holding out just two fingers on principle instead of his whole hand." Azad uses the German for 'subhuman', *Untermensch*. He speaks slowly, measuring his words, groping for the appropriate German word or phrase, which he's fond of slipping into the conversation. "This country has no qualified people," he declares, sweeping his arm towards a dhow casting off from shore. "The bosses were all teachers, bookkeepers or engineers before they were made chairmen of multinational corporations. They function only with the help of their senior managers and can't speak English properly because they can't be bothered to learn it. But Jordanians speak Arabic and English so these managers are generally Jordanian," he says. Azad removes his sunglasses and fixes me with narrowed eyes. "Jordan is Palestine," he says, darkly. "A bastard country with an army of well-trained sneaks." These managers wield enormous influence because they know how to quickly make themselves indispensable, he says. They ingratiate themselves with their bosses, lead negotiations with foreign businesses, play the movers and shakers to the outside and fawn their way to the top. "The Emiratis have relinquished their power to these people without noticing," says Azad. "Inter-Arab relationships are symbiotic and very binding. One has everything to lose, the other nothing. But among themselves, the subordinates make fun of their masters."

We wander through a labyrinth of vernacular houses on the waterfront, which were once the homes of wealthy Persian merchants. The roofs are punctuated by wind towers, rectangular structures that provided an early form of air conditioning by catching

the passing breeze and funnelling it into the rooms below. Bats flutter through the empty alleyways along with a solitary bird late home to roost. These newly restored one- and two-storey houses seem like a charming afterthought in the concrete jungle that has grown up around them, though they were in fact built at the turn of the 20th century. I wonder out loud why there are no people about at this time of day and speculate that the residents are all sitting in *majlises* behind their high walls, puffing on their water pipes. Azad lets out a guffaw: "There are as good as no Arabs here," he says. "The majority of those who moved in when the place was restored a few years ago are Westerners or Iranians. They appreciate the difference between a house like this and the typical plastic stuff in the city."

Through the other side, gaggles of tourists in shorts and sleeveless dresses roam the colonnaded souk and besiege the museum, which occupies the original little fort with its historic cannons flanking the heavy carved doors. Azad resumes his own story and he tells me how he deserted the Iraqi army on the mountainous frontline – sliding down a glacier on his behind, out of one mess and into another.

When we near my hotel he flags down a taxi and invites me for a drink. We end up in a Holiday Inn that has seen better days. Azad, it seems, is a regular. Barely are we through the door before a waitress pours him a beer and places it on a little table by a mirrored column, jammed between the bar, a billiard table with a group of cavorting young Russians, and a crowd of Indians following the cricket on a wall-mounted flat-screen TV. I sip a bitter-almond Chardonnay and find myself eyeball to eyeball with Charles Bronson peering out from a poster beside the dartboard. The wine makes me sleepy, which suits Azad well enough. He wants my undivided attention, though preferably without interruption. He pulls some photos from his briefcase. He has two little dark-eyed girls aged four and five from his marriage to a cousin in Baghdad whom he whisked away to Bergen. He seems to miss his little girls especially.

Before long, we are treated to the appearance of a flame-haired female singer with a chalky face and black lipstick. Someone has squeezed her into an ill-advised, narrow-waisted dress of patent leather. When she starts to caterwaul a Stevie Wonder number conversation becomes impossible. But the resourceful Azad has an idea and, for lack of resolve and want of a better one, I tag along with him on an expedition to the nearby BurJuman shopping mall.

At about three hundred metres long and at least fifteen years old, the BurJuman is small and venerable by Dubai standards but it's still thriving on the attentions of the internationally well-heeled. As they glide along the escalators and corridors of designer shops with their monster bags, an empty-handed interloper can be forgiven for feeling like a potential mugger.

Azad zeroes in on a fast-food joint and orders us lamb kebabs with french fries, which we eat from paper plates. I lean back in my chair and gawp at the merry dance of conspicuous consumption. BurJuman is popular with tourists and locals alike. There are Emiratis here too. Families with strollers and iPods, popcorn and soda, sashay by with mobiles dangling from their wrists, casting an expert eye over the goods on display at Louis Vuitton, giving the impression of being very much at home on this stage.

6 January
Is this city a city?

There are streets with no names, buildings with no numbers and addresses turn out to be directions given to the nearest landmark: a school, hospital or the inevitable shopping mall. Roads are upgraded and new ones built at such speed that a GPS system is of little use. Maps are outdated as soon as they're published and mine only roughly corresponds to the maze of new developments spreading fast as fungus over sand and land reclaimed from the sea. Still, it does at least provide some convincing evidence that a city exists.

The barren terrain to the far south-west is dominated by power plants and a vast container port said to be the largest man-made harbour in the world. Follow the coast north-east towards the Creek and you come across the densely packed tower blocks of a new marina. It's only half built but already has more skyscrapers than

Singapore. Drive on and you encounter a tangled web of overpasses and underpasses giving access to an offshore construction site where they're building a series of artificial islands arranged in the shape of a palm tree. Carry on along the coast road as it heads north-east, and you pass a succession of enormous pseudo-Arabian palaces, self-contained five-star resorts catering to the whims of mass tourism. From here you can see the exclusive Burj Al Arab. Billing itself as the world's only seven-star hotel, it is shaped like a spinnaker and stands on its own artificial island. On the outside it's all elegance; inside, it's Versace for the globe-trotting rich, in questionable taste.

From this point on, ranging along the coast and a few blocks inland over several square kilometres, are the leafy suburbs of Umm Suqeim and Jumeirah, an extraordinary biotope of garden villas with pools, all within reach of beach clubs, clinics, schools and supermarkets and home to prosperous, and predominantly white, expat communities. Tens of thousands of British, French, Germans, Dutch and Italians have migrated here, though close examination reveals tight little national enclaves, each clustering safely within the culture and customs of home. There are executives and entrepreneurs, bankers and brokers, running their own businesses or working for global corporations such as insurance giant AIG. Tax-free earnings and corporate perks take care of the school fees and rent, while stockbrokers nurture expanding portfolios and Filipina maids see to everything from the housework to the scallops in vanilla sauce for supper. It all adds up to a degree of affluence the residents here might never have achieved in their home countries, while affording them a couple of all-terrain vehicles in the drive and a lifestyle of luxury and ease. They send their kids to the same international private schools. They socialize at the stables or their poolside barbecues, the bar at the golf club or the swankiest of the myriad health and beauty spas – that is, when they're not taking extended trips home or flying to the Maldives or Seychelles for a change of beach. It's easy to reinvent yourself here, and they do. They'd never have made it this big if they'd stuck it out in Newport and Varese or Nantes and Nijkerk.

To the east of this neighbourhood and running parallel to the coast road runs the business district of Sheikh Zayed Road. This is the main arterial route in and out of the city and is said to carry not just the heaviest traffic in the Middle East but the most exuberant flow of capital. The big market players and the seriously loaded all have addresses in the skyscrapers here. It's a world away but just a few kilometres from my temporary home near the Creek in Bur Dubai.

Essentially a place of transit, Bur Dubai is the first port of call for the majority of new hirelings regardless of their continent of origin or which corner of the city they eventually fetch up in. Nowhere else will you find so many cheap apartments for short-term rent, nowhere else as many suitcases and boxes packed and unpacked. Unlike the regimented grid systems of the gleaming expat estates or the sleek modern highways that force you to choose your direction and stick with it, this is a haphazard place best navigated on foot; a warren of alleyways such as you'd find in Cairo or Baghdad.

Which, for a place in constant flux, turns out to be one of its shortcomings. The majority of people living here travel to other parts of the city for work and the narrow streets are choked with morning traffic. Its bad enough if you have a car and worse if you don't. You can wait an hour for a taxi, only to find yourself sitting another hour in gridlock.

But there's something different about today. It's Thursday, the end of the working week. My colleagues have relaxed their usual sartorial standards and swapped bespoke tailoring and designer ties for worn, colourful tee shirts with American college names emblazoned on their chests. The women wear their freshly coiffed hair down and have traded skirts and jackets for loose collarless shirts and frayed jeans. The Strategy Director wears his sunglasses hooked in the V-neck of his tee shirt. Even the conversation is more relaxed. The polite salutations and brisk acknowledgements of the past few days give way to spontaneous banter, and the lively chatter and eruptions of laughter of young men and women from middle management

echo through the 4th-floor offices, a hush falling only when an Emirati colleague shimmies by in his *dishdash*. There are only a few Emiratis on this floor of the building and their disdain for the Thursday dress code is conspicuous.

As chance would have it, I run into Mohammed while stepping from the lift, and to my surprise he invites me to join him for a smoke at a *sheesha* café on the piazza between the towers. He quizzes me a bit on the way and submits to my quizzing in return. I learn he has been living in a one-room apartment for seven years, has no time to furnish it, still drives the same little Mazda rental car and would like to marry but can't find the right woman. We sit opposite each other under a sunshade and watch the waiter load the little bowl of the water pipe with glowing charcoal. Mohammed reveals he is thirty-one, studied in London and at one time worked for a Middle Eastern investment company in New York. He knows the world, he says, and Dubai is the best bit of it, a sentiment he'd already expressed on the phone a few months ago. Garmisch-Partenkirchen, Bologna, Amsterdam: all fine and nice but everything in Europe, population included, is old, and anyway that's not the market we focus on here. The markets for him are the new ones, the proud emerging countries. Mohammed has a thing for China in particular, though apparently he has never been there. India is already in the bag. His pale brown eyes linger briefly on my right shoulder. I assume this is a habit, a sign he is speaking about something personal. The old world, in his emphatic judgement, will soon realize where the real centre of the universe lies. I hope I can muster such certainty the next time a journalist calls.

The minty taste of the *sheesha* is still tingling in my mouth when a colleague pokes his head round my cubbyhole door. Benson has been on his own here a while longer than I have and is aware of the importance of developing some kind of social life. I suppose there's no harm in letting him introduce me to the local nightlife.

We meet that evening at ten in an outdoor club with a sushi restaurant by the beach. Benson is an investment banker and responsible for Far East investors at Al Adheem. But he's also worked in Hong Kong and Frankfurt. His mother is from Hungary, his father from Indonesia, and the family has Swedish nationality. He was educated in Vevey, Atlanta and Singapore. Benson wastes no time in getting down to personal detail, divulging that he's pushing fifty and is currently in an unhappy if lingering relationship with a Korean woman living in Paris. He has little clue how to extricate himself but knows the clock is ticking. Benson is desperate to start a family and move to Budapest where he has inherited a large house on the Danube. For the past fifteen months he has spent most of his time shuttling between the 4th-floor office, this club, and his apartment on Sheikh Zayed Road where he can receive five hundred and sixty channels on his cable TV. He's constantly on the lookout but has yet to find a lasting and harmonious alternative to the

Korean, who visits for a long weekend every two months and usually ends up scratching his face in one kind of spat or another.

Glancing around, I wonder why Benson is having such a hard time finding a wife. The surrounding tables are gradually filling and the place is teeming with good-looking women between twenty and forty. Benson confides he's met a few he liked at first sight but admits he has been unable so far to sustain a relationship beyond a few weeks. The majority of women here are from Eastern Europe, and their goal is to marry as quickly and advantageously as possible to support their designer shopping habits. Benson gives the impression of being able comfortably to meet such needs but presumably has a more romantic relationship in mind.

This evening proves another lonesome one for Benson, despite our moving at midnight to the circular dance floor upstairs. We've joined a swarm of the cocktail tipsy with serious partying in mind and the music gets livelier and louder as the night wears on. At some point in the early hours I catch Benson's insinuating nod in the direction of four blonde girls who can barely have reached maturity. "Ukrainians," he yells at me. His wrinkled forehead is wet with sweat as he jostles against the bodies crowding in on us. "Waiting for sheikhs – foreign and domestic." The club's elite clientele will arrive incognito sometime later, he predicts. Sure enough, I spot the girls later cavorting with some young Arabs escorted by African bodyguards, their presence a silent warning to keep our distance.

By four in the morning I can hardly feel my feet and Benson seems content to call it a night. We pad across the newly sprinkled lawns to the exit, slowly recovering our hearing, and Benson confesses he wouldn't have thought it possible to spend an entire evening with a German without being bored or irritated. He giggles and I wonder if he's had too much to drink. Frankly, I feel I have contributed far less to the evening's success than he has and I tell him so. He gives me a sideways look and shakes his head. What he had previously failed to mention was that his grandfather was gassed at Majdanek. He gives me a consoling pat on the shoulder and summons a taxi from the waiting queue.

7 January

The question still gnaws at me: Is this city a city?

Last night's clubbing notwithstanding, the luxury of a long weekend lie-in is denied to me. I have a headache, of course, from the bitter-almond Chardonnay, but there's something else bothering me. In the cool light of dawn, while I ponder the likelihood of finding painkillers in the bathroom to throttle the hammering that's working its way up from the nape of my neck, I manage to pull it into focus.

The events of the day before yesterday scroll like a film on the blank screen of my mind. Walid from the PR department met me at the entrance of the Municipality Clinic. I was there to fulfill the requirements for a residence visa by undergoing a health test, obligatory for anyone wanting to stay here more than a few months. He took me to a single-storey barrack block and led me past a long queue of boiler-suited Pakistani and Bangladeshi labourers, waiting in line until summoned one by one to a door with a sign reading "X-Ray". The place reeked of vinegar and freshly polished linoleum. The men were waiting meekly and patiently. I, meanwhile, was whisked behind a partition where six trainee Filipino doctors awaited the likes of me. One stuck a needle in my left arm and extracted a phial of blood, as quickly and efficiently as a bottle-filling plant.

I drag myself to the bathroom and back. The film has ended but it poses the recurring question: Is this city really a city? If nine-tenths of the population is merely tolerated, accorded the status of guest but not of citizen, does it really qualify as a city at all? What does it say about a place when expats have to go through all this for a visa that allows them to stay only three years, before being required to leave or go through it all again? I resolve to stay in bed until the painkillers take effect.

There are scores of nationalities in Dubai and there are two: locals and foreigners. I can't say I've seen much of the former so far but it strikes me that both groups have something fundamental in common: an overriding desire to live in peace and prosperity. But if that's a formula for harmony, it also throws up anomalies. Although Arabic is the official language, English is the *lingua franca* of this new global city and for the majority it's not their mother tongue. Everyone speaks it differently, and to my ears the babel of voices runs the whole gamut of sound, from a funfair cacophony to the counterpoint of a musical canon.

When the modern emirate of Dubai was created after the British withdrawal from the Gulf in 1971, there was oil beneath the sand to last a few decades, sufficient to fuel the boom that catapulted this small coastal town into the 20th century. The city's rulers were smart enough to realize that other ways of filling their coffers would be needed when the oil ran out, and sought to attract the vital ingredients for continuing development and prosperity: foreign investment and labour. Within forty years the population swelled from 60,000 to 1.6 million. The economy grew by ten percent and more each year. When oil supplies dwindled, Sheikh Mohammed and his brokers conjured gold from the sand itself, every square inch promising prodigious profit. By the start of the new millennium the city was on a development high, devouring all the building resources the rest of the world could supply: cement, glass, steel, cranes, lifts and migrant workers.

Expats converged in their thousands, lured by a burgeoning market in which they could buy or sell their labour, goods or services under conditions more advantageous than perhaps anywhere else in the world. And yet the capital fuelling all this growth is mostly foreign capital, the people still outsiders.

Located at the interface between low- and high-wage regions of the world labour market, Dubai offers a new model of urban development, where a metropolis designed for the hugely wealthy is made possible only by a contrastingly poor migrant workforce. A Filipina maid and her European employer nonetheless have something in common: they are both transients, both foreigners here. It is not so much the roof over their heads that they share, but their joint status as foreigners on the move.

But the Dubai of today is not like the New York of yesterday.

There is neither the opportunity nor the incentive to assimilate. Contemporary migrants are not only wary of committing themselves irrevocably, but are unable to do so. Everyone here lives in a state of impermanence, prepared to leave at a moment's notice. This city has nurtured a new breed of economic nomad who, by choice or necessity, is constantly in transit, looking for the next big thing, as a way out of hardship or to get rich quick. Dubai's legacy to the cities of tomorrow will be its people – a generation of culture hoppers.

Still, my residence visa, however temporary, is now in the bag and it does confer certain privileges. I can buy a house, get an alcohol licence, and rent a car. Good reasons to get out of bed.

I enquire at three different car rental places before finding one that caters to my modest means. I hire a Polo and head out of the city on the highway to the point where the desert begins. Except it doesn't. It's lacerated by tarmac and roadside hoardings trumpeting a clutch of new developments: Business Bay, Dubai Land and Global Village. Plastic replicas of St Paul's Cathedral and the Great Wall of China hang from a metal gantry. A lonely bulldozer nuzzles the sand at a roundabout under construction and a lorry dozes abandoned nearby. From the look of things, Dubai Land and its cohorts might have come and gone already; man's tawdry ambitions surrendered to the elements, reclaimed by tumbleweed and the wind-blown sand.

The road swings south in a wide, sweeping arc and I find myself escorted by fleets of cement mixers and heavy construction vehicles. I wind up on the beach near a power plant in a bleak industrial zone, miles from the tourist resorts up the coast. As I paddle my feet in the gentle surf the sea suddenly takes on a grey pallor and a light rain begins to fall. Farther out, a small boat with a large Emirati fisherman bobs about on the water. He stands massive, with bulging belly, gathering the ends of a net fanned out below the waterline. Ten skinny Indians at the shoreline busy themselves frantically with the other end. They form a semi-circle, grab onto the net as well as one another and pull themselves little by little in the direction of the boat. Up to their hips in muddy water, they turn as one and haul the

laden net behind them. They toss their catch onto the sand and set to work pounding the hundreds of bouncing little bodies with a flipper. The man in the boat watches from afar, posture majestic.

But for the fishermen, the beach is empty until a Chinese couple wanders into view. The man is elderly and walks with a hunch. He has a go at hauling on the net but quickly gives up with a laugh. The rare warm drizzle proves no deterrent and two women in *abaya*s appear over the dunes with nanny and baby in tow. They're almost certainly related to the man on the boat but they turn their backs on the Indians, taking an exaggerated interest in the towers of Dubai Marina beyond. Joggers run by and slow down by the beached net where they trot on the spot in order to watch the lethal beating.

I wander north-east along the shoreline. Through the grey veil of cloud and rain I can just make out the monorail tracks and cranes at work on The Palm. Farther out, dredgers circle the site like a herd of curious hippopotami. Along the beach ahead, the dunes give way to level sand where a solitary fishing dhow shelters under a *barasti* roof. The rain begins to soak my shirt so I take a seat in the boat and look out across the grey, corrugated sea. A helicopter passes by, flying low and dragging an advertising banner behind it: Giving Life to Your Treasure (Dubai and Gulf LLC). There is not a soul here besides me. I wonder who's paying for that promotional brainwave.

The rain has died away. A shaft of violet light pierces the grey cloud and sunlight spills onto the beach ahead. My thoughts drift to my log cabin in the woods at Clausthal. I've caught myself daydreaming of it a lot recently, particularly when Fatma has left me alone in the cubbyhole when she goes off to pray. I try to distract myself with other fanciful ideas. An opera house … the programme offering *Cosi fan tutte* today and a Lebanese dance troupe tomorrow, followed by a performance of Cirque du Soleil, a modern Peking opera, and a Bollywood musical. Naturally the auditorium of my imagination really does fulfil the criteria of a true cultural melting pot.

11 January

In the past few days I have been summoned three times to a meeting with the President of Al Adheem. On each occasion Mohammed has stuck his head round our cubbyhole door late in the afternoon to announce that Marwan Al Hindawi will see me at eight the following morning. Each announcement is followed by strict instructions as to how I am to conduct myself and I am told the president will want concise answers and no digressions. Mohammed also wants a pre-meeting with me so he can "better understand" my ideas. Better? We've not had the merest exchange of ideas so far. And, at this rate, we're not likely to. The pre-meeting doesn't happen and Mohammed still has no idea of what I have to report to the president.

We draw a blank on the first two appointments, standing around for an hour outside Al Hindawi's office without so much as catching sight of his secretary. Mohammed does manage to reach him eventually on his cellphone but the lively conversation that ensues comes to nothing. On the third occasion, even Mohammed fails to turn up.

But I get a surprise at lunch today. Mohammed calls in a state of high excitement as I'm working my way through a chicken *shawarma* in a Lebanese restaurant in the Business Tower basement. I am expected on the 52nd floor in ten minutes. I am to meet the President along with a number of his colleagues who head other property development companies. I abandon my *shawarma* and make for my office where I hastily gather up some papers I'd collected at my meeting with Azad and Cecilia, along with a few slides and drawings illustrating comparable projects in other cities, and take the lift to the floor where it's rumoured the government has offices.

The first to arrive, I dump my papers on a coffee table and cross to the window. From up here the view is of an army of construction vehicles and diggers diagonally beneath, burrowing at least twenty metres deep into the sand. In the distance, cranes shimmer in the midday heat.

Time passes before anyone else shows up. Mohammed is first, talking into his mobile, with another young Arab in tow in an expensive suit that must be at least two sizes too big for him. He is carrying large-format boards with artists' impressions of Arabian palaces in a canal-side setting, which he mounts on easels ranged round the room. Mohammed gives me a nod. He is still on the phone.

Two more Arabs, foreigners not locals, arrive in quick succession, nodding in brief acknowledgement before withdrawing to a corner where they whisper together and check their Blackberries for messages. Mohammed is disinclined to chat. He is apparently unsure about what is expected of us and only gives vague answers to my questions. Finally the room is enlivened by the arrival of five men and two women in national dress. They are all in their early forties and greet one another enthusiastically in a jumble of Arabic and English. I am greeted last and perfunctorily and am invited, along with everyone else, to take a seat.

The atmosphere is particularly convivial now the Emiratis are here. Even Mohammed is in animated conversation with one of the women. He actually laughs. I can see it's costing him some effort, though. He's not on his home ground.

There's a flurry of the customary mobile telephoning and adjustment of headdresses by the men with close-cropped beards. And there's quite a bit of joshing too, one of their party the probable butt of the joke. The women interrupt to scold them but I'm at a loss to understand what's going on, not that anyone seems concerned or even to notice. At length, a giant enters the room. Well over six feet tall and broad in proportion, he greets everyone with a laid-back mumble of Arabic-English. He is the only one to introduce himself to me. He is clearly the highest-ranking individual here and I suppose he's the one close to the ruling sheikh that Benson has told me they call "The Boss".

The Boss has a booming delivery and a subtle smile that plays at the corners of his mouth. He asks how I like the city and I make a few friendly observations. His gaze drifts restlessly, making me feel I'm taking up too much of his time and attention. In the end, he sinks into a slightly raised leather chair and announces without preamble that the ruler has decided the city must become a centre of culture and that we – he gestures around the room – are the team to make it happen. I'm not sure if it is a coincidence but I alone am sitting on his right side on a capacious sofa. Mohammed's eyes are on me.

With that, The Boss introduces me to the others. The male Emiratis are all presidents of government-controlled corporations while the women work for the ruler's office. On The Boss's left is Al Adheem's president, Marwan Al Hindawi, my own elusive supervisor, who blinks at me with a mixture of embarrassment and mistrust through the tiny lenses of his spectacles. I give what I hope is a friendly nod and nervously straighten my papers and laptop on the sofa beside me. Mohammed's Arab assistant is the only one who hasn't taken a seat. Instead, he stands behind Mohammed maintaining eye contact with Marwan as if awaiting a signal.

The Boss launches into a short speech. The ruler, he tells us, recognizes the importance of strengthening the culture and education sectors. This is part of his overall strategy, in consequence of which The Boss envisages international auction houses relocating their business here, stars choosing to make the city their home, as in Hollywood, and the building of museums and theatres. Now it is up to us to implement the ruler's vision, he declares, sweeping his arm in an inclusive gesture. "As of today, you are the Cultural Committee!"

There is no time to be awestruck, however, because at that moment one of the Emiratis starts a muted conversation with ... well, himself, or so it seems. He holds his cellphone above his lap like a consecrated wafer, cables hanging from his shoulders, half-hidden under his *ghutra*, presumably using an earbud.

No one seems perturbed by the man's antics on the phone and Marwan seems to feel his big moment has come. He gestures casually to Mohammed and his assistant, who attempts to set up an easel in front of The Boss. But before he can complete the task, The Boss waves him away with a snort of laughter and a comment to the others apparently about Marwan, much to their amusement. Mohammed's assistant retreats and The Boss turns to me and asks how I imagine the cultural complex. The Emirati is still on the phone.

Feeling Mohammed's nervous eyes upon me and catching Marwan's ambiguous expression, I suddenly feel under incredible pressure, as if the agenda for the coming months might be set in the next two minutes. I speak of the wide variety of nationalities in the country and the task of taking their interests in music and theatre into account in a programme of Western and non-Western art. I ignore the blue plastic bag performing aerobatics outside, behind the heads of the Emiratis sitting with their backs to the window. When I hand him some data on international conservatoires, The Boss rises briefly and straightens his *dishdash*, in the manner of a woman adjusting a tight skirt.

Pressing on, I cite the example of a young Chinese pianist born at a time when there were no pianos to be found in China after the Cultural Revolution and who, twenty-five years later, is now one of the world's most famous and successful interpreters of Chopin and Schumann. My speech over, The Boss asks why my concept foresees merely a small stage for theatre, a large one for opera, and a concert hall. He recalls cinema planners making the same mistake in the 1970s when they built only a single auditorium, and then along came the multiplex with twenty-five screens. The same mistake must be possible with opera! I'm too stressed to see the funny side and in a way I'm grateful to The Boss for this interjection. Cinema versus opera! I just grab the opportunity to point out that there is art that turns a direct financial profit (cinema) and art that produces indirect profit, not to mention spiritual enrichment (opera). Movies funnel money directly into the coffers of the cinema, while opera generates indirect income that benefits many businesses and the entire city. But only when the government puts its money where its mouth is.

Much murmuring ensues in English and Arabic. The Boss wants more about how much it will cost. Mohammed gestures to Marwan in a way I can't interpret but which seems to be important. Two billion, he says then, and again I spot the tension in his eyes. "Make sure it stays at that," The Boss says, ominously. Then he remembers me mentioning that performances would not be possible on some evenings because of rehearsals. "Not in this country," he booms humorously, looking around to check the reaction of the others. "Breaks may be acceptable in other parts of the world. In Dubai, people work." And, as if to emphasize the point, he stands up, gabbles his farewells and strides out of the room.

Cue the arrival of another Emirati who introduces himself as Salem, from The Boss's office. He can't be more than thirty and has fine, almost feminine features suggesting a more Indian than Arab origin. It seems his job is to take care of me, though he doesn't say as much. We stand by the window and talk about my first week in the city and at Al Adheem. I tell him that in an opera house everyone keeps to the same libretto but in an investment company there seem to be several performances going on at once. His Delphic response is that Europeans and Americans tend to think about what might be done differently, while Arabs think about how you can do the same things better.

I had expected Mohammed to stick around for a quick debriefing and to have the chance at last of a face-to-face chat with Marwan, but it seems they have more important things to do. Salem suggests a coffee downstairs in Starbucks so we take the lift. Several floors down the doors open to reveal Marwan, who steps in and, in a manner suggesting he'd been waiting for me all along, joins in our discussion. Fumbling with the cable of his earpiece, he casually asks how expensive it is to run a theatre in Europe. Launching into an explanation about it having a lot to do with the size of the house, I get half way through when he turns to Salem and asks him something in Arabic. More passengers crowd in, jostling me closer to Marwan, who looks down on me from an advantage of at least half a head. Such proximity seems to make him more talkative, and he tells me about a trip to New York when he stayed on Times Square and saw a performance of *The Lion King*. "We should do things like that in our place in Deira," he declares. "We had a fat old Italian out here last year singing at an open-air auditorium near the banking district." I confirm I'm familiar with the singer's work; he's one of the great

men of international opera. He throws me a hesitant look through his tiny specs: "You mean that yowling is opera?" My bemused expression escapes him as he hurries from the lift in a blur of pinstripe suits.

Salem doesn't let on how he feels about Marwan. We order a coffee and take two armchairs in a corner. Like all his compatriots, or the ones I've met thus far, he fiddles with his *ghutra* now and then, with slender fingers that have almost certainly never been introduced to a shovel. It dawns on me that this is my first real encounter with a local.

He reaches across the table to hand me a business card, and even with my limited experience of Dubai I can see he's from a prominent family with considerable interests in hotels and automobiles; the name adorns innumerable advertising billboards across the city and I suspect he is close to the ruling family.

Salem, it transpires, studied marketing and has experience of the industry. "We know we have to sell our products in a way that appeals to people abroad," he says. He speaks with pride tempered by diffidence, and his enthusiasm for the progress his country has made in the space of twenty years is mitigated by a doleful expression that invites sympathy and understanding. "But marketing communications is one thing; art is something else," he says. "I am aware of that … despite the people in Marketing appointing a Director for the Arts." His shoulders heave in a fit of silent laughter and his mirth is like an omen. For the second time today, I have a feeling that something of great significance is happening, something that will affect the course of things in the months ahead.

Salem has heard that singers can be difficult but would like to meet some anyway. I imagine an opera singer carries the same mystique for him as someone in a *dishdash* might for me, and tell him that artists in everyday professional life are generally modest and well-mannered, as long as they are allowed to work without interference. Yes, they might hanker for audiences and admirers but in that respect they are probably no different from company presidents. Salem allows himself a conspiratorial grin. He speaks of his personal ambitions: one day he will own his own cinema showing the entire canon of auteur films from East and West from the 1950s onwards. Next to the cinema will be a bar with decent live music. We talk about the Abu Dhabi museum projects. Now everyone is jumping on the art and culture bandwagon, he says, but so far not much has happened. He makes the point with an Arab proverb: "The tongue has no bone." And then he says: "There are people here, many people, who say piano playing comes from the devil's fingers. And you're going to have to convince them otherwise."

13 January

With the exception of Thursdays, the frantic early morning activity in the Al Adheem office continues apace. I emerge from the lift every morning to be greeted with the customary friendly wave or nod through frosted glass as I make my way to Fatma, and I go on spreading the usual surprise and bewilderment when asked what I'm doing here and where I did it before.

But I'm attracting a different kind of attention from the old homeland, thanks to a photo of me on the internet taken among the glittering facades of Sheikh Zayed Road by an opportunistic photographer, who'd originally come to snap pictures of raspberry glacé and manzo brasato at a chef's summit in the Towers. My little cubbyhole is flooded with calls, emails and job applications. Arabists want to discuss my views on the role culture has to play in building an open society in the Gulf, artists and curators inquire about working for me, and art collectors, advisors and lobbyists attempt to convince me of the valuable contribution they can make to my "mission".

It is as if I've been split in two: the perplexing "cultural director" in the office, and the stellar cultural pioneer at home. I am a paradox; a mythical beast concocted from the erroneous perceptions of others – a unicorn.

15 January

Salem calls me by my surname when emailing me and by my first name when we meet, as we did last night when he invited me out for a *sheesha*. The restaurant had been transplanted from 16th-century Oman – an Arab-Portuguese fort with red carpet runners and flickering candles on high pedestals by the door. Inside, there's a hall with about fifty tables and a stage where musicians and technicians are preparing for their performance.

The headwaiter, resplendent in a folkloric outfit of pure panto-mime, flings his arms wide in florid welcome and begs us to choose a table. We're spoiled for choice – being the only customers. Salem settles on a table by the stage with a view of the musicians and we sit under the uncomfortably bright halogen lights. Before we've had a chance to order, the band strikes up with an ear-splitting chord on an electric guitar, and plays to an imaginary audience of ten thousand fans. My diaphragm vibrates in time with the drum kit. I shift my expression into neutral for Salem's benefit. I sense my lack of enthusiasm comes as no surprise and that he judges this might be one local experience too far. His customary languid mien has turned glum and his lower lip droops. A singer with mirrored sunglasses makes his entrance and yells something horribly guttural into the microphone. Salem stands up and signals me to follow. Outside, he says: "The right place, perhaps, but the wrong time." He has an admirable knack of rendering me speechless.

The promised *sheesha* never materializes. Minutes later we're in Salem's Wrangler Jeep, stuck in traffic. An hour of stop-go motoring later, we arrive back at my hotel having hatched a new plan. Salem wants to introduce me to a few artists, even if I do have less to do with the visual arts than with music and theatre. There may be barely any musicians in the city, but artists there are.

16 January

Behind the Porsches and Ferraris in the glittering showrooms of Sheikh Zayed Road lies the former industrial district of Al Quoz, a buffer zone between the ceaseless noise and brashness of the city and the quiet backwaters of bedouin dwellings and camel herds on the desert borderlands. It's an undistinguished area of garages, warehouses, factory outlets, import–export businesses and labour camps. It's also an area of cheaper rentals and low-cost housing for less well-off locals. As a result, it has acquired a bohemian cachet and attracts the likes of young photographers, graphic artists and website designers along with the more adventurous expats. Here, on the wrong side of the tracks from the money, is where you'll find galleries representing some of the most successful Arab and particularly Iranian artists.

Salem and I bump down a sandy alley in his Jeep, past modest, single-storey, occasionally whitewashed dwellings secluded behind high walls. Exuberant hibiscus spills out of the tiny gardens while elderly Mitsubishis doze in the heat. And then there's a sight you rarely see in Dubai: half-naked children playing football in the street. Salem pulls up outside the Sailing House, the exterior distinguished only by the trunk of a large mimosa protruding from the wall and wound around with coloured twine.

This is the home of Hassan, the most distinguished of all the Emirates' artists. No one knows for sure how old he is, Salem tells me; he could be sixty-five or fifty, but here he is venerated as the wise old man of art.

We ring the bell and a recessed door swings open behind the wrought-iron gate. A young Indian escorts us to a small interior courtyard where we meet two men, smiling shyly, both in jeans and tee shirts. The one wearing a baseball cap steps forward to greet us and introduces himself as the owner of the Sailing House. In another life, Abdul-Hamid was a banker, though it's hard to imagine now. For the past few years he has given over his residence for use as an artists' retreat, representing the tenants who stay there rent-free. Hassan was his first guest and he uses the place to paint and store his works, hundreds of which had been stored in containers on the roof of the building. They number in the hundreds and have been multiplying recently. Hassan, it appears, is very prolific.

Abdul-Hamid explains all this hurriedly, as if I have more important things to do than listen to him, while he leads me past oil paintings and glass showcases stuffed with various *objets trouvés*. As he reaches a closed door he breaks off suddenly and looks across at the other man, who until now has followed in silence. So this is Hassan. He has more than a little grey hair, a comically spherical paunch and a bushy, cigarette-stained moustache. Peering through wire-framed glasses, he bestows a gaze of deep melancholy on everything he sees. And when it comes to seeing, he takes his time. So we stand regarding one another wordlessly for quite some while.

Salem, unfazed by this and after a suitable pause, turns the handle and opens the door to the tiny room that Hassan calls home. There are three chairs, a wallpapering table, a bookcase – on which I spot from a distance a copy of the interviews between David Sylvester and Francis Bacon – and an unmade bed. Hassan is first across the threshold and from the ceremonious way he ushers us inside you can tell he doesn't get much company. Abdul-Hamid leaves us alone.

So here I am with the sage of Emirati art, who started drawing at the age of eight, who in the late 1950s or early 1960s attended the only school offering drawing classes and found himself an outsider for his lack of interest in sport, and who later became a caricaturist. He was probably able to get away with it then, when the country was so busy constructing itself that political criticism went unnoticed or at least unremarked. Such work would almost certainly be more controversial today, and censored.

Throwing back the bed sheet, he spreads out his most recent work. It looks like a jumble of statistics to me: numerical values and squares, diagrams divided in segments, each barely distinguishable from the other. Hassan calls it the semi-system, a schematic of order and chance. He learnt all about improvisation in the early 1980s in the jazz clubs of London, when he was a student. His influences include Russian Constructivism and the Bauhaus. Hassan is gaining momentum, lighting one cigarette from the end of another, reeling off opinions about Paul Klee and Johannes Itten, Wittgenstein and the Frankfurt School, and brandishing essays he wrote on the

Bauhaus in Arabic. The time will come, he says, to publish an anthology and he already has a title for it: *Pluralistic Position*. The air conditioner hums, drawing the dense smoke of Gauloises into a swirling pall above our heads.

We climb the stairs. "Colour," declares Hassan, "is colour, nothing more. Red is just red; it doesn't stand for anything, not blood, not war." And the word "red" is nothing more than the noun for the coloured pigment. He's no fan of symbolism, nor does he like inventing words. Hassan simply *makes* art. The little rooms we pass through on the way upstairs are littered with bits of packaging, gaudy hair combs, flip flops and boat shoes, strewn about the floor or on shelves like recumbent sculptures, or dangling behind panes of glass – Hassan's response to the glittering city.

The upper storey houses a small studio where there are two dozen or so unfinished paintings, representational images in vibrant colours depicting men in suits with furious faces standing in front of microphones, cows at pasture with tomatoes hovering in the air above them, the night sky over the flat roofs of Al Quoz. Hassan opens a door onto the roof. The surrounding houses are no more than two storeys high, their flat zinc-clad roofs festooned with lines of washing, turreted with water tanks and vent stacks and sprouting the odd tuft of vegetation. Hassan remarks on the dense clusters of satellite dishes. He's taken a shine to them. They are a connection to an invisible world. "The heavens above us," says he, "are full of invisible signs and signals that determine our lives." That's something artists and satellites have in common. They transform invisible signs into words, colours, people and pictures. He's working on a series of watercolours right now, abstract rhomboids dedicated to the satellite dishes.

As I'm taking my leave, Abdul-Hamid appears at the top of the staircase and leads me back out onto the roof. He gestures towards a rusty, dented oil drum. "If you want to understand what it means to be an artist in this city," he says, "you have to know the history of that drum." Hassan interjects that he shouldn't be digging up dirt from the past. But Abdul-Hamid won't be silenced. He has a bee in his bonnet. Blinking furiously, his voice rising with bitterness, he carries on: "A little over thirty years ago, Hassan unveiled this barrel at the local art society as one of his first works. The people were outraged and removed the drum on the night of the opening. Newspapers the next day condemned characters like Hassan for not being artists but sorcerers who should be burned." Hassan, increasingly impatient, is tapping Abdul-Hamid on the arm and shaking his head in disapproval. He tells Abdul-Hamid he should leave these things be, that everything has gone pretty well since then. "Pretty well?" rages Abdul-Hamid. "Things are going terribly!"

Abdul-Hamid has apparently got things off his chest for now. I shake hands with Hassan and he holds mine in his own for a while, as if he means to add something. But he limits himself to a benign smile that somehow suffuses his mournful eyes. We make our way down the narrow staircase without him. Abdul-Hamid pulls self-consciously at the peak of his baseball hat. He's not finished after all. "Ministers and sheikhs have shown up at exhibitions in this city," he says. "Hassan is fascinated by the moment these people stand in front of his work, completely at a loss. Ministers can't understand work like this. And as soon as they realize that, the work is all worth it to Hassan. And to me, too."

We're standing under the mimosa, whose trunk Hassan has encased in gaudy cotton twine, lending the courtyard the look of a children's playground. "The neighbours are giving me trouble," whispers Abdul-Hamid. "Why don't I go to work? Why don't I rent the house out instead of filling it with useless pictures?" He breaks off and starts speaking to Salem in Arabic, which he then translates for me. Someone has pressed charges and the Municipality is threatening penalties because the Sailing House has illegally added a room to protect the oil paintings from the heat from the roof.

Back in the car, Salem comments: "Do something that people don't understand and there will be trouble. Art that doesn't turn a profit, for example." That knack again – I am lost for a ready reply.

17 January

How astounding that the country's most important artist finds it necessary to hide from his neighbours. And if his artworks are fashioned from the city's detritus and profitless daydreams then, presumably, he must hide from an entire city. But those idealistic dreams I nursed when I first arrived here are not so easily negated just because they are founded on possibilities, not present reality. It's just that the more I see of the reality, the further the possibilities seem to recede.

I suspect Salem, my unexpected companion, was deliberately trying to put my confidence to the test. He may have been briefed explicitly to do that, though it's possibly just a consequence of his natural seriousness and candour. I wonder if The Boss selected him for that very reason. Salem is just the type to sound out someone like me who is soon to be involved in the company's internal affairs.

26 January

Working with Azad on plans for the theatre building, I feel we're beginning to understand each other. I take it as a sign of trust that he shows me the original brief given to the architects so I can see how it has developed. Initially, there were plans for five auditoria (one of them a concert hall), a museum (at the wish of the ruler's wife), and a hotel. The preliminary design has been revised and we're now down to two auditoria – the larger one to seat three thousand – and a hotel intended to defray the costs of the culture business. Given the company chief takes Pavarotti for a caterwauler and *The Lion King* for opera, this is probably a wise decision though it's still adventurous to the point of reckless when you consider the average volume of a singer's voice and audience projections for the next ten years.

The Boss's new Cultural Committee has not met since it was appointed but Mohammed holds a weekly meeting with me, Azad and Henry, a corpulent Australian in charge of the overall planning for the Deira complex. I present my arguments but fail to convince them that an auditorium for three thousand is incompatible with the natural laws of acoustics and that a smaller space is what is required for opera. I am the sceptic on the team. How, I ask, is a so-called six-star hotel supposed to cover the cost of a year-round cultural programme?

My first month here is drawing to a close and it is a case of more haste, less speed. Completion has been pushed back from three years to five. Azad says the construction sector is completely overheated. There are 800,000 working on Dubai's construction sites but there's still a shortage of manpower and the complexity of the design will almost certainly lead to problems during the build. I try to find some consolation in that. Buildings may be made to order but culture requires long, painstaking nurturing.

My business model envisages a transition phase during which people become gradually accustomed to regular opportunities for listening to classical music before anyone attempts to fill a large new auditorium. Initial performances intended to instill the classical music habit might be held in some kind of pavilion near the construction site, on a theatre ship, perhaps, or a large raft anchored in the Creek.

The idea isn't exactly received with rapturous applause, but nor is it rejected out of hand. Henry, who for some reason has taken to fiddling with a set of prayer beads like a Muslim, shrugs. Nevertheless, the decision is made to take on a ship for a trial.

2

2 February

My phone and email in the past few weeks have been buzzing with talk of theatres and concert halls. My correspondents are architects, contractors, impresarios and agents and they all have the same story to tell: they are working with a local developer who has been granted a plot of land by the ruler. The developer is trying to determine the various components of the property he is to build. Strategy consultants have told him that a gallery, museum or planetarium would be advisable; a theatre would be even better. This kind of facility offers "added value" to a development and is a surefire "marketing tool" for selling the apartments, office space and hotel capacity that will form the bulk of the development and generate the essential profit.

The Emirati property developer may know nothing about art or culture, but he does know about competition. He knows the ruler has offered his cousin a plot of land adjacent to the one he wants to develop. The winning developer will be the one with the plan that most pleases the ruler. Which of them will it be? For the developer, this is the critical question. He has to come up with something that trumps the competition and so he takes his strategists' advice and plans a theatre, gallery or museum. Analysts conduct research on the world's great cultural institutions. But their findings are vague. So how do these places cover their costs and make their money? Which company, for example, supports the Louvre, La Scala or the Metropolitan Museum? In most cases the answer is support from the state or from charitable donations – not the answer required. The developer grows impatient and instructs his strategists to inquire of the institutions themselves. Many of those contacted are either baffled by the questions or are suspicious. A property development company from the United Arab Emirates? There are some who need to look the place up on a map.

Never mind, the strategist already has his eye on a more attractive model: Las Vegas, for instance. Here he finds confirmation that a theatre can be run like a proper business. The developer invites representatives from the various entertainment companies to Dubai, shows them master plans, extols the skyrocketing population and tourist count, the favourable investment conditions, the unrestrictive business structures in the free zones. The representatives are impressed. Nowhere else can the industry be developed so easily and with so little regulation. What's more, the developer gives the impression of dealing with exclusive rights by way of a mandate from the ruler: the city's "theatre" is to be built on land already granted for the purpose. The representatives from the West, impresarios, media entrepreneurs and music agents, bring their expertise to bear to prove to the developer that, naturally, one theatre will not be enough. In no time at all they produce figures for other international cities where they are working on comparable musical venues, theme parks and entertainment centres. Once again the developer considers the competition, which is not just his cousin now but the rest of the world. He will only really impress the ruler by building theatres and theme parks of a whole new magnitude. What's needed is more square footage and more visitors than anywhere else under the sun!

The developer and Western entertainment companies come to an agreement. A contract is signed to the tune of several billion dirhams and thousands of seats. Projected visitor numbers are estimated in the millions so that the investment can be refinanced without delay.

After closing their respective deals, two impresarios meet by chance in the breakfast room of one of the city's luxury hotels. They know each other and start chatting with a little less reserve than they usually might. They are surprised to learn that each is here on the same mission.

I know all this because sometimes people take me, mistakenly, for the person pulling the strings. And Azad's employee Cecilia has proved herself to be an astonishingly capable analyst, collecting a wealth of data and industry gossip. In the space of seven days she has identified sixteen theatres and twenty-four museums and galleries in the pipeline. She makes no claims for the list's exhaustiveness.

This strikes me forcibly as news of vital significance, and for once I call Mohammed in the evening on his mobile and suggest a meeting with Marwan and The Boss. Mohammed won't hear of it. It is the ruler's will that all projects be developed in competition with one another. Culture can be no exception. I shouldn't worry about the others; instead I should ensure the speedy success of our complex. As if it were up to me. I explain why we should not try to compete with Universal, DreamWorks or Cirque du Soleil. Our complex has a different profile. There are altogether too many cultural developments being planned without a clear business case. For some incomprehensible reason he seems happy at the news. Clearly, I have failed to get my point across.

Which is why I tell the story to Salem and suggest a new organization that would develop culture as a whole in the city, or at least co-ordinate it. This seems to amuse him. "You Germans always want to keep things under control," he laughs. "Here, there just isn't any." Once again, I am tongue-tied.

8 February

A journalist calls to congratulate me on my appointment, which might be deemed unprofessional elsewhere, and says he'd like to interview me. I have nothing against it though Mohammed failed to respond to yesterday's repeated request for the promised press release, choosing instead to bawl someone out on his mobile phone before holing himself up, self-satisfied, in his office.

A German TV crew telephones. It is Friday (the weekend) and almost nine in the evening (they had forgotten about the time difference). They want to speak to me about my billion-dollar projects. They also want to know if it would be possible to film construction sites and interview the ruler. I deflate their expectations and try to compensate, mostly by making myself available. I also warn them sternly against planning any filming without the requisite permit, which can take up to two weeks to issue. Questions follow in rapid succession about traffic jams, foreign workers, tourists and the artificiality of all this development and whether, under such conditions, cultural development is even possible. They have a point. And they also have me nicely by the tail. I expatiate on the ruler's emphasis on education, the loyalty of his subjects, the development of a society that is both Islamic and tolerant. I remind them of the neighbours that the people here are dealing with, Iran and Pakistan, for example. I even throw them a line comparing ambitions in the Gulf today with the achievements of the European Enlightenment. I have to cradle the receiver. It's not first time in recent weeks I've made such claims. The ruler another Louis XIV? Well, maybe he is – I've yet to meet him.

15 February

As some great thinker once asserted, "Time is *now*" – meaning that time exists only in our experience of the present. So how do you find time in a place that is intent on fleeing the present and dashing headlong into the future, where everyone's got his foot down on the accelerator in relentless pursuit of the next thing – with the exception of the Deira Complex planning team?

I recall my first few days here when I had the luxury of boredom and could drift aimlessly on the beach and down by the Creek. I see myself outside the hotel the day I arrived. It all seems so long ago yet it's only been six weeks.

I remember standing in that busy street in Bur Dubai wondering

if it was a place where it was possible to say one had actually arrived at all, feeling an overwhelming sense of the relentless pace of it all … seeing it all simultaneously, in a single discrete moment: standing motionless as people hurtled past from one air-conditioned zone to the next, the ground moving beneath their feet, construction cranes swinging their wide arcs day and night, hands clutching glasses, grasping telephones and reaching for banknotes. No, no one ever arrives here. This is a city in frantic motion. It's not just a race against time, it's an objection to it. The people here really do live 24/7. Everything is in transit, taking off, on the move. People live and work on the go; they earn money on the go and spend it on the go. They love, hate, desire and mourn on the go. It's one giant souk peopled with soldiers of fortune, celebrities, lifeguards, imams, and air traffic controllers. They see one another and look past one another. The city is a jumble of races with a myriad voices. The talk is incessant, but nobody's listening.

18 February

The monsoon winds are blowing. The morning call to prayer has barely sounded over the roofs of Mirdiff and Nad Al Sheba and sailors are hauling the sleek wooden hulls of their racing dhows and catamarans onto trailers. They set off in Landcruisers and Armadas and Avalanches, leaving the skyline of Sheikh Zayed Road behind them as they head for the open beach.

Local men in white and grey *dishdash*es with dark skins and African faces shout instructions to a troop of Pakistanis spreading sails on the sand. The beach is otherwise empty, but for the sand-pipers teetering along the shoreline. It is too early for swimmers.

Curious gulls dance round the boats squawking at the men as they hammer and fix the sails and call out to one another in Arabic, Hindi and Urdu. The spinning wheel of a bogged-down Jeep tosses a fountain of sand to the rear, making it look every inch the raging steer about to attack. Portraits of Sheikh Zayed and Sheikh Mohammed adorn side and rear windows of vehicles parked in the dunes, the patriotic zeal extending to brand new BMWs spray-painted with the UAE national flag. Streamers and ribbons play in the breeze.

The sailors hustle their onshore crews, shouting and urging them on as they push the boats over the last few metres of sand and into the turquoise surf. They want to be out on the water before the heat gets up. They head out towards the billowing sail of the Burj Al Arab. Beyond is the trunk of the Palm heading out to sea, and at the end of the causeway rises the pink Disney palace of the Atlantis Hotel. From this angle, it looks like a locust poised to jump.

I'm jumping ship. I've had enough of my cheap hotel apartment in Bur Dubai and decide after six weeks it's time to move on. Returning to this dingy hotel apartment every evening has fostered an increasingly insistent delusion that the dark-stained furniture and beige easy chairs are growing larger and it won't be long before the suspiciously worn, though admittedly odourless, furnishings finally overwhelm me. They conjure up ghosts of previous occupants and I can't help wondering what's gone on between these walls since they

were built twenty years ago: a British family man on a construction job far from home, having a go at a girl on the coffee table; an Indian door-to-door salesmen in cheap but perfectly pressed suit, relaxing with a few bottles of beer, staring silently at the cricket on TV; a father and son from the Jordanian lowlands, visiting a cousin who has found the son a job as a post office clerk, father in bed, son asleep on the couch; this apartment connecting the unknowable fates of a thousand restless souls. The gloomy corridor outside, by contrast, offers nothing but carpeted silence. And if you did happen to run into someone, it would be an everyman with a face resembling all the faces behind those anonymous doors. It would be a face you forgot the moment you saw it.

My new apartment hovers 250 metres above the highway. I am the first tenant up here and, judging by the workers I meet in the lift and the noise they produce on the floors below, I'm living in a fifty-storey construction site. But the apartment is fresh and bright. There's water and electricity and, typically for Arab houses, an ensuite bathroom in every room.

Standing next door is a steel-and-concrete block that threatens to rob me one day of my unparalleled view of the Gulf, city and desert. It's growing like the mythical beanstalk but it won't spoil my outlook for a while. At five in the evening, the red disc of the sun sinks through a fogbank over the sea. Refracted light transforms it into a spinning top, sliced horizontally by a thin layer of cloud. From this height, the Gulf looks like a pink Persian carpet with its patterns of man-made islands and buildings. And when the fiery orb of the sun is finally extinguished the misty carpet rises like a mirage and hovers over the sea.

Now I can sit in my own chair by my own coffee machine and sleep in my own bed, I have regained a sense of calm. There are people who choose to sleep rough in cardboard boxes or spend their holidays camping in tents. Not me. I need a home, even if there's not much to it. I've seen pictures of people who return to homes destroyed by earthquakes, just so they can tend to the vegetables still growing in what was once the front garden. I think I'd probably do the same.

21 February

I've got into the habit of going into the office for a few hours on a Saturday to answer longer emails. This time, I arrived to find the 4th floor completely cleaned out save for the grey carpet runners. A sheepish Indian security guard shrugs his shoulders. Going from room to room, I find not a single sign that my colleagues in the strategy department were sitting there just the day before yesterday. It's only in my cubbyhole that the desk has been left with all my things: the usual office supplies and a satellite picture of Deira, with a little red arrow indicating the location of the new theatre complex. In what was once the photocopying room, the sole survivor is one of the company drivers, pottering about with a trolley and several reams of paper. The man speaks only Urdu and indicates his need to call someone else who might help me. I think of calling Mohammed, but ring Salem instead. He shows up at the Tower half an hour later and we meet at the scene of our first encounter, in Starbucks.

Salem has news. His office is setting up a team to co-ordinate cultural development, at the government's request. It was all decided the day before yesterday. Salem has The Boss's ear, and when he informed him of the plethora of theatres and museums so thoughtlessly planned for the city, The Boss turned to him and said: "Then you take it over, you and the German." Salem says the The Boss mentioned something about a "Task Force", which has an unnervingly military ring to it, but I keep such reservations to myself. I'm elated that something is happening at last and in the excitement I even forget to ask what has happened to the Al Adheem management team.

Salem withers my new-found enthusiasm with a pitying look. "It's not exactly a *new* work group," he says. He's been working on an urban culture concept for a few months now with a couple of young Emirati women (from prominent families) who have recently graduated from a course in design at the American University. Besides, this is the third attempt at formulating a plan in the past five years. And big ideas come and go: an Arab Medina with high-tech entertainment, a 21st-century oasis, co-operations with the Louvre and Covent Garden, a Venice in the desert, a Hollywood on the Gulf: they've all been on the drawing board. "The problem is not that no one has any ideas, but that they have too many," says Salem. "It's not that The Boss doesn't understand anything; it's just that he's inundated with proposals."

Which is where the Task Force comes in. With me, apparently, they'll feel more confident they'll be protected from proposals …

Now I've installed myself in a nook by the window in the office formerly belonging to Marwan and am preparing for two young Emiratis to move in. And Carmen Gonzales. According to Carmen, she is one of the few Indian secretaries (or personal assistants, as they are called here) in the Emirates Tower who speaks Arabic. Salem pulled her from the 52nd floor.

Carmen was lured here from Mumbai by the increase in salary.

Her son and daughter have grown up in the fifteen years she's been here but she's still supporting them, her mother and a disabled sister, all of them a three-hour flight away and living back home in a house she managed to buy from her savings a few years ago. She started out working in the oil industry but eventually tired of being chauffeured back and forth across the desert between the refinery and her office twice a day. So she took a government job where she worked her way through various departments including public health care, accounting and marketing. Her features hint at her Goan origins, with skin the colour of coffee and a wide face with a generous mouth, large flattish nose and small, dark wide-set eyes. She is barely five feet tall and, despite having a few years on me, not a single grey hair on her head, though I'd guess she's put on a few pounds since her youth.

Carmen's Hindi accent takes some getting used to and the peculiarly discordant timbre of her voice packs a powerful wallop in a room empty but for our two desks. She seems to be aware of this herself, to give her credit, and thankfully tones it down to a more moderate level. On our first morning together she confides she would live in Switzerland if she could. Rain and snow are the greatest gifts you could give her. As I explain my background and tell her about my work here she nods, a little confused yet assertively, the way people do when they're keeping their guard up. She won't be drawn when it comes to music and theatre and has a subtle way of masking her insecurity. If she's not familiar with a name or doesn't know the context, she wrinkles her brow and looks to me to, as it were, jog her overloaded memory.

22 February

Latifa and Mona look alike to me. Maybe it's the *abaya*s or something about them being the same age. They laugh a lot and are generally much more approachable than the local women I've encountered so far. Neither has ever set foot in a theatre; the visual arts are what turn them on. Mona was born in Hamburg where her father studied and later worked as a doctor. Her sisters speak German, but she only spent the first two years of her life there so remembers nothing of it. They've visited the great museums in London a few times and would like to see something similar here one day. Latifa calls herself an artist, and bemoans a state of affairs that makes it necessary for a female from a respected family to first create the conditions for a suitable profession, before other women are permitted to follow and earn their own money.

The two monopolize the front area of the office with their Louis Vuitton and Yves Saint Laurent handbags, various mobile phones and computers. No sooner are they installed than the room resounds with their rasping tones in a never-ending, recitative duet. Later that afternoon a convoy of couriers arrives to distract them with umpteen boxes containing scores of drawings and oil paintings, some of them colossal. My new colleagues direct each other in the hanging and positioning of their artworks and throw me an inquiring look. I attempt a compliment. They are, for the most part, awkward and naïve productions rendered in neon colours. Their parents allowed them to paint only because they are women, Latifa blurts out. Mona lets out a peal of laughter, imagining her brother holding a brush in front of a canvas. Clearly, nothing could be funnier. It all became possible, apparently, when a daughter of the ruler started showing her paintings at private exhibitions. His Highness attended an opening and proclaimed that art was not only beautiful, but important for future generations. Breaking cover as an artist has been acceptable ever since.

3

3 March

What was once an office has been transformed into a playground, with me as single parent at his writing desk, watching his offspring carry on. Carmen is usually visited by colleagues from the upper floors between 9 and 11 o'clock, when she discusses options for the lunch break. Her greatest worry is timing her departure in the afternoon in order to miss the notorious rush-hour traffic. Latifa and Mona usually arrive at around noon, looking very tired. Each day, the young ladies have new artworks dragged into the office, which they pile on the only clear table in the room. It seems a very serious business so I stay out of it.

The rest of the 4th floor seems to have spawned a host of new government organizations. There are temporary signs on office doors reading: *Women's Establishment*, *Authority for Knowledge*, *Intercultural Office* – new government babies in the tender care of predominantly female Emiratis preparing for final exams in politics or public administration. Our space is turning into a kind of office-hours recreation centre. The women all prefer to congregate here, probably because of the entertainment value. By late afternoon they're swapping lipsticks and eyeliner pencils, exclaiming over family photos and touring the personal art collections, all to the accompaniment of profuse laughter.

As for the Task Force, it seems I am it and I'm crafting a theatre

complex with several stages and a museum that will gain Dubai the status of a world laboratory of global culture. Salem drops in from time to time and shares a joke with Latifa and Mona if they are there, or sits with me if they're not and enquires about proposals he's sent for my evaluation. He assures me he will give the young women something to do when the time is right. He leaves me in the dark as to when that might be and I don't push it. I have learned that Emiratis open up more the less you ask. Something will happen; I sense it in Salem's slightly abstracted expression.

8 March
Some time ago, our neighbouring emirate of Abu Dhabi startled the international culture community with news of plans to open franchises of the Louvre and Guggenheim in the capital city. The review sections of the world's press were abuzz with reports of financial investments so gargantuan it seemed irrelevant what currency they might be in, and of star architects unveiling their proposals with the aid of elaborate models and presentations. Up till

now the Western world had viewed the Middle East as oil producers, a market for fast cars, a breeding ground for Al Qaida, and the home of robed and veiled peoples with supposedly outdated attitudes when it came to culture. At a stroke the Abu Dhabi announcement called this hoary old cliché into question. Now, suddenly, it was: "Not only do the sheikhs want our money and our cars, they're also after our art!" Was nothing sacred? Were there no parts the tentacles of oil income could not reach?

The resulting controversy was at its fiercest in France where the government was accused of organizing a cultural sellout. The furore soon died down. It quickly became apparent that the deals would provide an income stream for the institutions involved and the majority of works on display would, in any case, be those currently in storage. The hook was baited. Other European institutions came up with ways of drawing attention to themselves with cultural platforms such as fairs and festivals and forums dedicated to the Middle East. Auction houses and galleries considered opening branches in the region, specialist logistics and insurance companies offered their services and analysts, and consultants sought to cash in with in-depth regional studies.

The terms "culture" and "desert" had once been mutually exclusive propositions. Now the sand had transformed itself into one great big friendly expanse where the entire world could store and display its history and its treasures. The Western mind loves a paradox and here was a barren wilderness offering itself as the repository of the highest achievements of mankind. The possibilities ran riot in the minds of certain cultural professionals of the avant-garde. How exciting it would be to start afresh, in a world still virginal, with no tradition, no legacy, no cultural premise!

Just how such a new beginning might look takes protean shape from the blizzard of submissions pouring in daily. They amount to the Gulf region being targeted as an entrepot for whatever the rest of the world can't use or is beyond its means to buy or supply.

I flip through photo albums showing ice sculptures of the ruler or the Burj Al Arab; technical drawings for subterranean entertainment labyrinths, designed to mimic computer viruses; and proposals for sumptuous coffee-table books on old and new masters, with advice on what is currently available on the market. And a never-ending stream of job applications: from curators, former secretaries of rock stars, lighting experts, holders of large dinosaur collections, and the authors of exotic "art world" tours for the QE2. Were it not so wearisome, I might feel a certain pride in the West's surplus of creativity.

Paper is patient and can be left in the in-tray to wait, unlike visitors. I have to ask Carmen to turn more and more people away at the lift as they've now sniffed out the location of the largely unpublicized Task Force. I tell her to take their business cards and promise to get back to them. She collected twenty-seven yesterday, only thirteen today. For the most part people are just travelling through and stopping off to pay a courtesy call and make contact, even though strictly speaking I'm only supposed to be helping Al Adheem build a new theatre and have no authority to act in any official capacity. Others want to discuss "interesting ideas", which are confidential, of course, and can only be shared with me face-to-face. I'm beginning to appreciate Salem's comment about needing to be protected from people and their ideas.

I spotted two turtles in a pet shop window and adopted them immediately. "Bought" would be an inadequate description in view of the unexpected surge of sympathy I felt for them. They are imported from Florida. They were cosying up on a rock in a little aquarium and when they stretched their long, stripey necks they seemed to be nodding at me. I couldn't resist. My first turtles. The aquarium, which I purchased on the spot, stands in an unused bathroom in my apartment and measures almost two metres long, though the little creatures themselves can be held between index finger and thumb. The salesperson told me this would soon change and that both are female. They don't like the dry food as much as the little shreds of smoked bresaola ham I buy at my local Spinney's supermarket. They only become active after sundown and under artificial light, which reminds me of my opera days. And they like to go foraging in and around the water.

9 March

Latifa met him a few months ago at the Women's University. He had professorial ambitions and impressed her so much she gave him my mobile number and suggested he give me a call. The professorship was never awarded but his enthusiasm for the city remains undimmed. Ken is from Gothenburg and is a little over six feet tall. His shaven skull, parchment skin and the dark rings under his eyes lend a kind of fragility to his otherwise powerful appearance, as does his thin little castrato voice. He wears a black tee shirt with his own likeness on it (printed in black), military trousers and combat boots. If you want to Google him, you have to put his name in quotation marks. I know that from Latifa. The reason for her fascination is immediately obvious. This is how, informed by years of PlayStation fantasy, she imagines an artist should be. Ken, who is in his late thirties, seems to see himself in the same way, because from the way he tells his story he might have come here by way of a swashbuckling Viking cartoon.

It begins in Berlin in the early days of techno after the Wall came down, with ear-splitting clubs for those in the know in cellars, factory buildings and World War II bunkers. Night after night, an international community of ravers seeking physical and chemical oblivion would thrash about to diabolical synthesized noise in the laser-pierced gloom. They'd rave into the early hours until sweat dripped from the walls and then shuffle home through the waking city, smoking one last joint. This was Ken's natural milieu. But at some point he grew weary of it all and resolved to become a businessman. He bought some companies in Russia and, by his own account, enabled a number of people to become millionaires and billionaires through his ideas. He now specializes in buying and selling internet domains and owns a number of top-level ones with "Dubai" in the name. These are his capital; he has sold several already to local organizations and businesses.

Ken's stare is intense. I should know, he tells me, that he feels a deep affinity with the country's ruler and his vision. It was the invitation to "think big" that struck a chord and drew him to the Gulf from the cold (and clearly cash-strapped) cultural wastelands of northern and eastern Europe. He feels they are kindred spirits and it is the subject of one of his paintings. It's too big to carry round, obviously, but happily he has a brochure to show me with photos of his work. There are interior shots of a "centre for intellectual and creative consultation" that he built on the Baltic coast in Lithuania. I see colour photographs of offices and conference rooms, of the kind you might find anywhere here, only more expensively furnished. Ken's work hangs on the walls, large-format oil paintings in greens and browns, which I take to be an expression of their creator's spiritual world. The style is consistent throughout. It's how I imagine a painting might look if you used a pack of assorted mongrels as brushes and got them to roll on the canvas. Ken is thinking of presenting his artwork to the Sheikh and proffers another photo. This time it's a montage of Ken and the ruler standing in front of his piece, *Think Big*, which is five metres high and features a giant caramel caterpillar crawling across the middle. Ken is wearing a *dishdash*, though his is somewhat less magnificent than the Sheikh's. The Sage of Gothenburg has already learned much about the Arab world, and I venture a compliment to that effect. Thus emboldened, he suggests another big idea: ten sculptures, five hundred metres tall, to be placed strategically throughout the city. All the sculptures render a Big Thinker in steel. Ken has a scaled down model in rubber, which he fishes from his messenger bag. The Big Thinker has copied his pose from Rodin, but looks more like Batman in a sadomasochist's outfit. Ken wants someone to help put him in touch with the Sheikh. I promise to inquire on the 52nd floor.

13 March

His Highness Sheikh Mansour from a neighbouring emirate wants a word. We agree to meet in the lobby of the Emirates Hotel. The young man in the powder blue *dishdash* cuts a cool and elegant figure as he sits, hands folded in his lap, amid his entourage of black-clad Arabs in this air-conditioned milieu of minimalist luxury, peopled with Kuwaiti oil traders, platinum-blonde supermodels and discreetly hovering Indian serving boys. He has typically sharp bedouin features, with aquiline nose and close-set eyes. I take a seat opposite him on a turquoise leather sofa and he rests his dark and unwavering gaze upon me. Salem, who had informed me of the Sheikh's bidding, is not in attendance, though he did brief me that His Highness's métier is the international design business and that he has plans to open his business headquarters here. He's said to be in cahoots with the ruling families, has an interest in cultural projects and an idea for a design centre. A few short months' experience of this strange new world have already attuned me to the distinctive whiff of Arab politics.

Sheikh Mansour and I pass the time of day about the unique challenges of working in this city. He knows the place well, despite spending most of his time in Florida and Switzerland, and believes the centre of international creativity is shifting to the East. Individuals like himself have much to contribute to the development of a modern Islamic identity that combines the best of Western art and Arab culture. It is time to return to Arabia, he says. He name-drops various well-known Arab poets, fashion designers and pop musicians, all good friends of his currently living in the West but waiting to make this city their new creative home. Then, as if further discussion along these lines would be tedious, he casually switches the subject to his new design centre. "High-end" is Sheikh Mansour's buzzword of choice.

He inquires politely about the new Task Force's strategy and I admit that we are still in the conceptualizing phase, concentrating mainly on the complex in Deira, adding how important I think it not to take on too much at once, so that I'm pushing for an evaluation of plans already on the table. I tell him about the clueless developers who want to build theatres and museums without knowing what cultural enterprises are for and try to sum up my ideas for provisional urban platforms for the arts. He listens to all this without comment then closes in for the kill: The Boss has suggested that he give me an impression of his project. He gestures to one of the three silent Arabs comprising his entourage then reaches over to hand me a DVD.

I promise to get back to him, a little taken aback that Salem has failed to brief me on this new proposal: a centre to feed a city of three million culture-starved inhabitants with a campus for the arts including a cinema, a theatre and a college of art, fashion and design. It turns out that the square footage proposed is roughly that of the Louvre and nobody has taken the trouble to disguise the fact that the project was originally designed for another city in the Gulf. The location map points to a strip of coast south of the emirate of Dubai and the project still bears the name of its ruler.

Sheikh Mansour's centre of art and design is also a commercial concern, naturally. In fact it's *mostly* commercial: eighty-five percent of the space is given over to "shopping, drinking and dining". The attached business plan (investment: 550 million US dollars) suggests the remaining fifteen percent (in other words the arts projects) will be financed by profits from the rental business. I zap through a gallery of "exclusive" labels and fantasy fashions: exotic and andro-gynous fourteen-year-old models in lascivious poses, dunked in neon paint and attired in diaphanous Indian fabrics; 3-D extravaganzas from digital media outfits advertising their skills in cutting-edge animation; a local mineral water supplier presenting its plastic bottles in a dramatically-lit photo suggesting some connection between their contents and the moon; all this accompanied by a collage of sound, the likes of which you might expect had Brian Eno converted to Sufism. In the last chapter I stumble unexpectedly on the Deira masterplan. Sheikh Mansour's project occupies the same spot as our cultural complex as indicated on the Al Adheem maps.

The next day, Salem remains insouciant as I fill him in on my encounter with His Highness and my discovery. He says he knows the idea of planning several competing projects on the same plot of land seems unusual from a Western perspective but people have a different approach here. Don't worry about it, he says. The important thing is that I met Mansour. No one will be bother me further with his ambitions. That's another local custom.

14 March

I leave the highway in a depression in the dunes, taking advantage of an opening in the otherwise undamaged wire fence meant to keep the camels off the road, and use an air gauge to check the tyre pressure on the SUV I have rented for the weekend. I follow a reliable-looking trail through the dunes and drive westward. The lower the sun sinks, the stronger the wind blows. Swirling sand streaks across the car and dances in glimmering spirals over the track. Darkness falls faster away from the artificial lights of the city. I should have made camp sooner. A hollow between two twenty-metre-high dunes seems to afford shelter and I pitch the tent quickly as the sun sinks below the sand-blown horizon.

Half an hour later the wind has dropped and it's pitch black and about ten degrees cooler. There is nothing in my surroundings to indicate civilization though I'm only a few kilometres from the highway. I lie down, my back warmed by sand that still retains the heat of the day. The vast and star-lit canopy twinkles with such brilliance and clarity I could be in a planetarium. Satellites wander across the moonless sky, against the majestic turning backdrop of the constellations. The moon rises and bathes the desert in white light, the hollow of my campsite resembling a giant's footprint in the sand. A commotion rouses me from my reverie – it turns out to be an inch-long beetle near my ear. In the distance, something is moving, maybe a mile, maybe only a metre away … I seem to see it snaking and crawling, but by now I'm in the Land of Nod, under a different sky.

I dream of a grinding escalator in a mosque made of ice, from which I am retreating, shivering, and am jolted from it the next morning by persistent rumblings. My bleary eyes behold six camels, growling contentedly as they nibble the tiny tufts of grass beside my tent. The beasts are indifferent to the car, the tent and me. Evidently

they are accustomed to such things. I get up, feeling strangely weightless, and spot a *badawi* nearby, lifting his *dishdash* as he ducks into the dunes. The climbing sun warms the air and I pack up my belongings.

The *badawi* reappears over the dunes and I stop to offer him a lift. His face and head are wound with a headcloth as protection from the sun and rising wind and the only feature visible is a pair of surprisingly blue eyes. He looks no more than twenty. At a crossing, he signals me to turn right and we pull up by a group of corrugated metal huts with a few scrawny chickens running about. An electricity generator roars against the wind and there's an old Toyota pickup truck, loaded with wood, parked in the shadows. An old man emerges from behind a door and totters out to greet us. He has a long, snow-white beard that forks below his chin and a mahogany face scored with deep grooves like the cracks in the parched earth beneath his feet. His pale eyes gleam beneath bushy eyebrows. The boy calls out to the old man and disappears inside the hut, quickly reappearing and inviting me to get out of the car and take a seat on one of two benches in the shade of a stunted little tree: an open-air majlis.

The boy speaks a little English and tells me his name is Yusuf. His father's name is Abdullah, and the current ruler's father called him "Lassar", which means something like *Reliable One*. They ask if I am from London, like most of the whites. The old man, nimble on his feet now he has a visitor, fetches a stack of three little bowls, arranges them on a low table by the benches, and pours a hot drink fragrant with cardamom. We sit sipping our coffee in silence and I succumb to a pleasant languor. All is quiet but for the rumble of the generator, the sound of the breeze and the occasional clucking of a hen. The old man waves a hand in the direction from which I came and pulls a mobile phone from his pocket. The boy tells me he'd like to exchange numbers. They visit the city sometimes to go to the camel races. Yusuf tentatively taps my number into the phone and calls me so I can save his number. Surprisingly, we get a connection out here.

That taken care of, they resume their silent contemplation of me. Though it's not yet 9 o'clock, it's beginning to get hot and I decide to make my way back. The old man grasps my hand and tells me via the boy that the Almighty will join our paths again.

Finding the route back turns out to be easy enough, and not far from the opening in the fence I come upon a filling station where I can pump up my tyres. After half-an-hour's driving I approach a bridge over the highway with a billboard trumpeting: *The Sun Never Sets on Dubai World.* The diggers are already out working in the haze of the rising heat; the octopus of the city is invisible beyond the horizon but it's extending its tentacles as I press on to the rhythm of construction vehicles, cranes and the unceasing traffic.

18 March

I've received two calls already in the last three days. The boy asks if

I'm doing well and when I am coming back to the desert. I promise to come soon, though whether I could find the two again without help I'm not at all sure.

19 March

My doorbell rings at about 10 p.m, for the first time ever. I'm not expecting anyone but, having already come to the conclusion this is a safe city, imagine it's nothing to get exercised about. The door opens to a haggard-looking man with sparse, white hair who is probably only in his early fifties. He fiddles awkwardly with his wire-framed glasses as he introduces himself, making it hard to look him directly in the eye. He says, with a gesture in my direction, that he too is from Germany and works as an independent consultant for an acoustics company. He's heard of the cultural complex and the enormous task I've taken on here, and wants to hear more about it and maybe apply to work with us. Pulling his wallet from his jacket, he hands me a business card.

Wrong-footed at first, I play for time, and ask how he found me. Apparently a photograph of me in a magazine helped reveal my whereabouts. He compared the view from the window of my apartment in the photo with the city skyline and managed to identify the building that way. My visitor confirms with a smile that the receptionist in the lobby gave him my apartment number.

It's a tricky predicament. The man wants something from me and may well have something to offer – he certainly has plenty of nerve. I resist the urge to tell him he must have lost his mind if he thinks turning up at my home at this hour is the way to commend himself. Instead, I put his card in my pocket and, with admirable self-restraint, advise him that we certainly won't need experts such as himself in the short term and, in any case, I am not the person responsible for construction. I am beginning to sound like a broken record on this point; it's a phrase I find myself repeating in emails and phone calls every day. But I know it's better to remain courteous than risk an ugly situation developing, so I wish him a diplomatic

لقد علمتنا الصحراء أن نصبر طويلا حتى ينبت الخير وعلينا أن نصبر ونواصل مسيرة البناء حتى نحقق الخير للوطن.

Desert has taught us to wait long periods of time until we see green plants. So we have to be patient and resume our building process in order to achieve the nation welfare.

good night and close the door, feeling that I have only narrowly succeeded in defusing the situation.

20 March

Meetings are still being convened, if only occasionally, with Mohammed, Henry and Azad. During the most recent, Henry suddenly throws his prayer beads on the table and roars with laughter. Carmen, who takes the minutes, is barely able to conceal her contempt and looks at me dumbfounded. She doesn't like Henry. He is crude, unreliable and arrogant, and is having an affair with his secretary. And when he laughs he exposes his brown, broken teeth, which Carmen likes even less. But Henry has good reason to be amused. He informs us that the budget for the cultural complex will probably be only 560 million US dollars and not the 900 previously estimated. According to him, each of the various budgets neglects to include costs for different components of the building design. The biggest problem is infrastructure. To make the complex accessible to three thousand people there will have to be a large subterranean car park and a feeder road built over the Creek. Besides that, there may well be complications with the new metro connection. Counting everything together, the total would have to be at least two billion. The cost of building the cultural centre itself represents just a quarter of that total budget. Nor is it the fault of the star architect, infra-structural implications not being his problem.

Henry knows the ruler has already announced the project and therefore has little choice but to see it through. So he takes the budget news in his stride. But his next revelation has him snorting with laughter: "Do you know what they're calling the thing?" he asks, "The *Oprah House!* – O.P.R.A.H," and he jiggles his prayer beads again, chuckling to himself.

Two billion! These days, a budget that size would be more likely to be associated with the reconstruction of Iraq than a cultural complex. Perhaps it's all part of Henry's plan. Perhaps he's secretly hoping the associated costs will make the opera house too expensive to ever be realized. My former colleague Pink, director of the New York Met, comes to mind: his opera house now broadcasts live performances worldwide via satellite. If opera is ever to have a chance here it'll be with the help of the Met. All it will take is for someone to get the ball rolling.

Apparently, the technical part of all this is pretty simple. Pink promises to put us in touch with his technicians.

22 March

The US President is coming to town. Since last night, we've been receiving information that suggests the government has all but declared a state of emergency: schools, services and construction sites will remain closed for the duration of Bush's visit. There's vague talk of roadblocks. No one has been told what time the President will arrive in the city or when he will leave.

Clearly, it would be better to stay at home today. But I can't afford to, because I'm taking my first business trip to London to speak with the architect and his engineer about various problems of space allocation in the plan for the Deira complex. I called the airline yesterday to check its limousine service would be available to pick me up today as arranged and received confirmation. Today I read in the paper that the Sheikh Zayed Road is closed. But I have to cross it to get to the airport! From my window I see the roads are deserted. There's not a soul to be seen, anywhere. It's as if someone has triggered a neutron bomb, all life obliterated. The presidential convoy will be rolling down the highway, looking out on dead houses, dead streets and dead plazas. There'll be none of the ceremonial pomp or crowds lining the protocol mile waving their little flags, and of course none of the dignitaries pressing the flesh and the photo opportunities that go with it.

Calls to the limousine service elicit only the engaged tone. I try repeatedly, to no effect. The newspaper lists the streets to the airport that are still passable. With some misgiving and a little more than five hours until my flight, I decide to abandon all hope of the limousine and set off to find a taxi. Standing outside on the empty street it feels as though I am the sole survivor in this forest of tower blocks. At this time of day the ten lanes of the highway are normally jammed with traffic, but today there's not a car to be seen. The friendly Indian concierge advises trying it with my own car. But I returned it to the rental place yesterday. The concierge insists that the taxi service refuses to drive into our neighbourhood. Our neighbourhood? I live opposite the government headquarters, for heaven's sake!

After another twenty minutes of fruitless effort to reach either the limousine service or Salem, I pluck up the courage to appeal to the only human being in the building that I have something of a social relationship with. My neighbour Khalil hails from Bahrain. He is no more than thirty-five, weighs about seventeen stone and always gives me a friendly smile when we meet by our front doors. Thankfully, he's at home, listens to me with concern and immediately declares his willingness to take me to the airport in his own car. We head out of the underground car park, which luckily has its exit ramp at the back of the building, so we can avoid the closed highway. There are a few vehicles out and about in the side streets, which is comforting, as are the temporary yellow signs indicating the route to the airport. There are, apparently, no other destinations today. At a five-lane roundabout, police guide us towards the only available exit. To my relief, it takes us over and beyond the highway towards the desert on the other side. I can tell it's not exactly the regular route to the airport, nor the one indicated in the newspapers, but the police seem to know what they're doing and Khalil is sitting confident at the wheel. He's tuned into a radio station, but there's no hope of a traffic report – it's broadcasting Hindi dance music. Stuck to his dashboard are portrait shots of various golfing legends – living and dead, as far as I can tell.

There's a long queue of vehicles waiting to get onto the next roundabout with drivers leaning from their windows bombarding police with questions about the road ahead. All the exits are barricaded with the exception of the one leading to the highway from which we've just come. Khalil mumbles something I don't understand and is suddenly galvanized. He switches off the radio, forces his ample frame out of the vehicle and grandly approaches a police officer, completely disregarding the queue of disgruntled drivers ahead of us. The constable shrugs his shoulders, grips the door of his four-by-four with one hand and shrugs his shoulders again. Then he yells something over to his people as Khalil climbs back into the car. We drive up to the barrier and, to my surprise, two policemen open it and allow us through to continue our journey on the empty road, towards the desert. There's no other vehicle in sight and we've just passed a sign to the airport, pointing in the opposite direction to the way we're going. Khalil is unconcerned. He barely talks and seems not to notice my growing anxiety. But his serenity has a calming effect. To the left I glimpse the farthest reaches of the Creek, a glistening pane of glass where flamingos gather in the salt marshes by a little forest of mangroves. So we drive around it and try to reach the airport from the opposite side.

At the next barricade, some distance outside the city, I show my

business card stating that I work for the government. Khalil assists and explains to the official that I have to get to the airport urgently to catch a flight to London. The man lets us through, though his shrugging does nothing to ease my anxiety. After ten minutes' driving – on the correct side of the road, as far as I'm aware – we encounter a group of motorists approaching us head-on, flashing their lights and gesticulating as they plough past us on the wrong side of the road; a few at first, then dozens of them. Khalil takes to the hard shoulder to protect us from the onslaught while he mulls things over. Even he is agitated now. Well, it's not something you encounter every day; hordes of vehicles bearing down, horns blaring and headlamps flashing. It's as if King Kong were up ahead, playing with lined-up vehicles, sweeping them before him and into our path. Maybe the President has crash-landed on the highway causing all this traffic chaos, I joke. Khalil makes a U-turn and trails the massed traffic offenders. They've spread out across all the lanes now and it's every man for himself. We turn off the highway and into a supermarket car park. At least there are a few people walking about here, as well as cars, circling circumspectly like sharks. Twenty minutes pass. I have completely lost my bearings now and ask no more questions; I am resigned to writing off my flight and attempt to persuade Khalil to find a café where we can wait until things calm down. But Khalil won't be defeated. He switches on the radio, leans back in his seat as far as a Mercedes 500 SL will allow a man of his stature, and puts his foot down.

Not long after, I stumble out of the car and onto the pavement outside Terminal 1. A group of Chinese tourists getting off the bus ahead of us asks how we got here. I'm not sure I know the answer to that myself. With just a little less than three-quarters of an hour until take-off, my goodbye to Khalil is a little less decorous than might be thought strictly proper in a country such as this: I sprint round to the driver's side and give him a big hug while he's still wedged behind the steering wheel, looking relieved and quite pleased with himself. In the departure lounge it's business as usual. The crowds jostle their way through security checks, check in their luggage, ride the esca-lators and scurry off to Duty Free. Departure gates are announced over the tannoy system and airport information boards flick into life announcing flight schedules and boarding times. No one seems remotely aware of the chaos outside.

That afternoon, heavy rain falls over the city as the President visits the British Embassy. Newspapers the next day will show him slipping on a wet staircase and almost taking a tumble. The locals have come up with a name for this auspicious visitation: Bush Day.

26 March

Destiny in the Desert is the first boxing match of any consequence to be held here, though enthusiasm for the new sport seems somewhat muted. About a hundred spectators gather at the 10,000-seat Zayed Hall in the World Trade Centre, the ring at its centre looking a bit lonesome. Most of the punters are Westerners, and by the way they sit, tight-lipped, in rapt attention, you can tell they are aficionados of such events at home. But there are locals here too, including at least twenty young women who seem not to be taking the thing very seriously, chatting to one another or talking into their cellphones. The first two fights, between dark- and fair-skinned Americans and an Ethiopian, suggest the financial compensation for an appointment with *Destiny in the Desert* can't be much more than a week's wage for a site foreman. Just before the third fight, a film is shown on a big screen in the grandstand featuring Emirati novice Eisa, who jogs through the dunes and speaks of his dreams of being a boxer.

The film pauses on a close-up of the sweating fighter facing a leather punch bag and Eisa waltzes into the auditorium to a hero's welcome. It dawns on me that this is the moment the women have been waiting for. Eisa performs the prayer in his corner and within twenty-five seconds his African American opponent is sprawling on the canvas, Eisa having thrown no punch worth the name.

The Emiratis go completely wild. While the beaten man is heaved unnoticed through the ropes, the ring fills with men looking like elves in their white beards and red-checked *ghutra*s. I peer over at the girls in *abaya*s. They're clutching one another in excitement, some with tears in their eyes. A baby is lifted into the ring and placed in Eisa's brawny arms. Finally the victor requests silence with an imperious wave of his hand, and launches into a ten-minute speech that presumably has something to do with the significance of this triumph for the future of the city.

A gaunt man with thinning hair makes a beeline for me as I'm leaving the auditorium. He's wearing a leather jacket and his face is flushed with the glow of someone genuinely stirred by the action we have just witnessed here. It's Bouman, a Flemish architect I ran into with Salem on the 52nd floor just a few days ago. I'm surprised to see him here (at a boxing match), and tell him so. He thinks I mean I'm surprised to see him in Dubai, and counters that he can think of no more exciting place to work these days. Not only is he an architect, but a person of wide curiosity too. While the hard-boiled boxing fans from the West talk shop, Bouman and I agree that the

city is interesting more for its people than its construction sites. Nevertheless, it's the construction sites, of course, that provide him with his contracts and afford him the opportunity to stay here from time to time.

27 March

A city awakes. Birds, plump and colourful, squabble in the branches of palm and bougainvillea in Jumeirah's gardens; hoopoes perch on fences, pecking at beetles and ants at work on the wood. Amahs drop their charges at the school bus; gardeners water the lawns and landscaped curbs. Traffic grinds to a halt on Sheikh Zayed Road and the clangour of steel from the construction sites rings out across the city; kestrels and plastic bags swoop through the polluted urban canyons of the business district; Filipino waiters lay tables in numberless hotels and restaurants; wage earners from all over the world, working for companies from all over the world, swing into office car parks, crowd into lifts, jostle on escalators, take up positions

behind desks and peruse the news wires and press cuttings for political and economic developments significant for their businesses. Freight is unloaded from turquoise-painted dhows on the Creek; a rising sun gilds the Trade Centre's rhomboid glass façade with its dazzling rays. The first of the day's tourists swarm through the markets of Deira, past stalls selling incense and gold. Buses rumble along the highway, packed with construction workers riding shoulder-to-shoulder to the next shift, their exhausted dark faces pressed close to the open slit of a window for air. Ukrainian girls ignore the racket of vacuum cleaners in the musty corridors outside as they dream of ending the day profitably in a young sheikh's place, after a day that begins in the afternoon on the streets and in the bars of Bur Dubai. Jet aircraft take off over the desert; passengers crane their necks for a final thrilling glimpse of the skyscraper skyline or sink back against their cushions, bored. The plane gains altitude and soars with the zephyrs far out over the Gulf. The Iranian coast meanders on the starboard side, but the pilot has other instructions and swings into his preordained route, to Shanghai, Düsseldorf or Cape Town.

29 March

Salem is at the lift to meet The Boss, whose powerful frame is today enveloped in a becoming *dishdash* of dove grey-blue. The Boss's stentorian greeting would be audible from the far side of the highway. He's about five years older than me, with a prominent jaw under the neatly trimmed beard – so neat, I notice, that it lacks even a single grey hair. His dark eyes glow like coals. "Yes, now it's really getting started," he booms genially, inviting my enthusiasm too. "I've been in training at Al Adheem for a while now," he continues, easing himself into the chair opposite me. I seem to detect an ironic grin flickering across his face; I cannot imagine he is unaware of how poorly Marwan is managing his business. "A new organization will be brought into existence in the next few days," he confides, fixing me with an ominous look. I am to work for the "Cultural Council", it transpires. I will be taking over as Cultural Director. Salem, who stands to attention behind The Boss and is now treated to an amused look from him, will be in charge of building the organization. "You will be given more people and all the support you need," The Boss promises. "I want you to flood the city with culture. In fourteen days I will invite you to a make a presentation of your strategy." I nod my assent and he and Salem take their leave.

It is probably no exaggeration to say that, in the past ten years at any rate, this man has made the city what it is. He started with thirty people in one of the ruler's offices and now runs an empire with forty thousand employees from all over the world, is a director of an airline and a group of luxury hotels, builds harbour facilities and tourist resorts, and oversees the banking business and the establishing of diplomatic relations. This man is the city. And we've been given the task of flooding it with culture. By building the Deira complex, for a start? Now, that would be something.

Salem returns with another instruction: a meeting in London with Sheikh Mansour and a Frenchman by the name of Matthieu has been scheduled for next week. The two, it seems, will be joining the supervisory board and will have instructions for us.

4

2 April

A mushroom cloud the colour of pewter rises above the skyline on Sheikh Zayed Road this morning; a djinn raising his steely fist to the sky. There is a fire somewhere out in the desert. At the office the news is that a warehouse full of fireworks has exploded. I wonder what, if anything, it portends for the day ahead.

Two hours later, Salem and I get out of the car, close to the mouth of the Creek. He heads for the entrance of a huge bedouin tent, made of pale grey canvas, where a group of young lads are waiting to greet and escort their bosses. Salem, Latifa and Mona have been working on this at fever pitch over the past few days. They even co-opted Carmen to send invitations, keeping me in the dark as though they wanted to surprise me. They have succeeded. The tent, equipped with a stage and rows of chairs, has the air of a movie theatre. A leading British marketing and public relations company has designed the programme, commissioned architectural models and produced a promotional video. I seem to detect the hand of the 52nd floor in all this.

Flunkeys roam the floor offering chilled and scented face towels, dates, celery sticks and orange slices. Brass coffee pots are placed on bar tables and lounge music plays from a loudspeaker. There are probably four hundred guests milling about, senior government employees mainly and friends of the ruling family. There are about fifty foreigners at most. A slide show of sepia-toned historic photos of Dubai is projected onto the walls of the tent. There are pictures of dark emaciated bodies diving into the shimmering waters of the Creek, retrieving pearls from the depths, their nostrils clamped with alarming nose clips. Incense hangs in the air.

Word goes round that the ruler is on his way. Everyone takes their seats, the Emiratis at the front, the foreigners in the back rows. No instructions are needed. Everyone knows their place. The central seats in the front row are left vacant. The music fades, the slide show dims, and the guests all rise as The Boss makes his entrance from the wing of the stage to welcome the ruler who, in contrast to the other Emiratis, wears a multicoloured *dishdash*, the dominant colour a luminous dark blue. Sheikh Mohammed glances around the tent with a friendly, almost shy, expression and utters a quiet "Salaam" before heading to the upholstered seat reserved for him. One of his sons, The Boss and Marwan follow in his wake along with a few other dignitaries, some of them in uniform. Once they have all taken their seats, the walls of the tent are parted again and the Crown Prince rushes in, prompting the entire audience – but for his father, of course – to rise a second time.

The younger son takes up position behind a lectern. From now on, it is his name that will be associated with the city's cultural development: His Highness Majed bin Mohammed Al Maktoum is to be president of the Cultural Council. Carmen, who is sitting next to me, whispers that she, Salem and Latifa prepared the speech. She is very proud of this and I have to be careful not to show too little enthusiasm. The young prince is not much over twenty. Although I don't understand a word he's saying, I know that he is telling us that this new governmental organization will, under his leadership, make Dubai one of the most important cultural destinations in the world. Salem had told me that much, at least, on the way here. I can imagine the rest: Dubai has proved its creativity in many sectors, realizing the ruler's vision of a truly global city in all its activities.

Carmen translates the closing remarks in a whisper. Time is short and the clock is ticking. The ruler has empowered his son, by decree,

to turn the area around the Creek into the city's centre of culture. The museums, galleries and theatres to be built in the years to come will testify to the intellectual and artistic greatness of Emirati culture, for the city's people and visitors alike.

The earnest young prince steps down from the lectern to loud and sustained applause. The foreigners around me beam as they clap.

Then the tent is plunged into darkness before a light shining stage left gradually resolves itself into a desert backdrop as two men in *dishdashes*, representing bedouin, stretch and contort their bodies in a choreographed mime around a flickering 3-D animation of a campfire. A mournful melody plays from the speakers. The scene freezes for a minute or more before the image is snuffed out and two new figures emerge, stage right, swathed in a shimmering blue light, presumably representing the hazardous depths of the sea. The two men "row" between the oscillating laser beams, uncovering pearls the size of ping-pong balls before they too are extinguished by the darkness.

Again the tent is plunged into Stygian gloom. There's some

nervous coughing and a frisson of tension in the air. A screen is lowered over the stage. We're treated to a virtual helicopter flight along the Creek, over dhows and past skyscrapers, glittering gold in the evening light and reflecting the image of a falconer with bird resting on his arm. We swoop over the alleys of Deira, where clouds of incense rise from glowing coals and traders drum up custom. Then the architecture slowly materializes. What, just a moment ago, looked like a warehouse or multi-storey car park is now a Persian fortress. The wharf, previously teeming with porters heaving their cargoes on deck, is now the setting for Emirati families climbing out of Mercedes and Porsche Cayennes to saunter through palm-lined gardens, occasionally encountering the odd white foreigner. The helicopter turns and approaches the other side of the Creek, where miles and miles of development-ripe land dreamily awaits marble villas and yachts, exclusive malls and landing strips for private jets.

The helicopter flight calls to mind, bizarrely, the opening scene of *Apocalypse Now* and the video's soundtrack is not unlike the dramatic theme music of the weekly newsreels that reported on the darkest chapters of my own country's history. When the camera hovers at last by the only genuinely historic quarter of Bur Dubai, the scene is obliterated by a superimposed neon slogan: *Khor Dubai: The Most Comprehensive Cultural Destination in the World.* There follows a list of projects: museums … galleries … theatres … cinemas. I count seventy-two. Our complex is among them, at least. But now it's called Theatre Land.

Our presentation reaches its climax with a musical finale that owes much to Wagner's *Death of Siegfried.* The screen rises to a high-tempo countdown soft-focused by green smoke that clears as the lights rise, to reveal a fifteen-metre-long model of the Creek. Cue a pregnant pause.

Then the ruler rises with his entourage to inspect the model. Marwan stands next to him and speaks to him from one side, over his shoulder, looking rather nervous, his eyes even slittier than his spectacles. The ruler gives an occasional nod, pointing at some spot on the model, turning now and then to his sons or The Boss.

The viewing lasts no more than ten minutes, and then the ruler retreats along the red carpet on which he entered. The remaining audience of three hundred or so mill around the model, most of them in apparently good humour. A couple of local journalists try to find someone to tell them something about the Creek and the Cultural Council. Pulse beginning to race, I fight my way with Carmen to the model to see what the new Cultural Council has in store for itself. I find a lovingly detailed landscape of nice little houses with Persian wind towers, interspersed with a few skyscrapers overlooking innocent little boats sailing on the Creek. I scan the model for evidence of the multifarious cultural projects paraded in the presentation. But it differs not a whit from the kind of model one finds at the city's ubiquitous launches promoting housing developments with malls attached, where you can sign up for an off-plan apartment on the spot. The only remaining relics of the past on the Deira side of the Creek – its old godowns, wharves and souks – have given way to a huge resort of luxury apartments and tourist markets. So much for the The Most Comprehensive Cultural Destination in the World – it is little more than a marketing wheeze to sell off the Creek to the highest bidder.

I look around for Salem and find him preoccupied with other matters, standing chatting with a clique of lads from the office. I must look annoyed because he shoots me a look of alarm as I approach. Before I can say a word, he pats me on the shoulder. "It's all starting now," he says. "You're not a task force any more; you're the Cultural Counsellor. Our Mr Culture."

3 April

We moved this morning to a larger office on the 28th floor, exactly halfway between the 4th and 52nd floors. Initially, its size conveys the (false) impression that things might have improved as far as the technology is concerned.

But there are just two telephones, only one of which makes international calls. Our nearest fax machine is on the 36th floor, the copier, which we share with the other fledgling government organizations, is still on the 4th floor, and there is no scanner.

I've nabbed a bay by a window and behind a glass wall, which I hope provides some slight shelter from most of the chaos generated by the other ten workplaces in the open-plan space, which is partitioned only by low room dividers. But now I'm sitting in something resembling an aquarium, having to contend with the non-adjustable air conditioning which switches itself on immediately and blows cold air relentlessly on the back of my neck. Even when I close the door to the bay, there's no escaping the chatter outside and I can make out scraps of English in the constant flow of Arabic conversation: family problems, the pros and cons of second wives, the new Audi R8, Lancôme's anti-ageing range, and so on.

The team has swollen to include new members: Khalil, Yasser and Tarek, young men previously in charge of event organization in The Boss's office, whose valuable experience in this arena apparently qualifies them for participation in the work of the Cultural Council.

5 April

There are many in this city who rarely if ever come into contact with Emiratis and find it hard to imagine what such proximity as I have might be like. I have even been asked if I feel lonely as the only foreigner on the 28th floor. On the contrary, I feel beleaguered; by petitioners, journalists, lobbyists and local luminaries on the city's international scene, all wanting in on the act. I need help.

My new Emirati colleagues do indeed possess talent in abundance – for avoiding work. On his desk Khalil has erected a model of a Gulfstream G250, the family plane used for long weekends in London and Geneva. I've yet to meet him properly since he's currently busy taking intensive flying lessons. Tarek collects vintage cars and in his twenty-four years has already amassed thirty-seven vehicles. The oldest is a 1913-model De Dion Bouton, the newest a 1980s Buick Century V6 Turbo Limousine. Like many Emiratis, Tarek's facial features betray little pure Arabian lineage: he looks like a prince from the heart of southern India. The numerous cords dangling from his white *dishdash* lend him additional distinction. I gather he likes to spend the early afternoons strolling round the offices in the tower, passing round a big square album bound in green silk displaying photos of him posing with his acquisitions. Yesterday afternoon he took the opportunity to give our colleagues in the Knowledge Authority a guided tour of his collection. The garages are outside the city on the way to Abu Dhabi, and the drive there and back takes so long that I've decided not to count on Tarek ever being at his desk in the afternoon.

And what of Khor Dubai, this most Comprehensive Cultural Destination? It would be nice if someone could tell us exactly what our remit is in the creation of this millennial masterpiece. Salem vouchsafes no immediate opinion, but comes back to the question after mulling it all over for a while. I express the wish to have direct access to The Boss, as he does. Salem listens. At times like these he looks uncomfortable, as if he's wondering how to tell me my fly's been open for the past hour. We sit in my goldfish bowl and watch the sun sink over the Gulf as the traffic builds up on the highway. A crane with a bundle of metal rods in its sling swings in front of my window. At least something is moving, I observe to Salem. And suddenly he looks less embarrassed.

6 April

It has been announced that four property developers, Al Adheem included, have been awarded contracts to build along various sections of the Creek parcelled out under the dubious labels of Theatre Land, Heritage Village, Global Art World, and Culture Metropolis. Theatre Land and Heritage Village are shoreline developments near the mouth of the Creek. Marwan and his colleagues, whom I met a few weeks ago on the 52nd floor, are now having their shot at the Khor Dubai projects inside the Creek. They have just promised the ruler seventy-two new culture facilities. With the exception of the Theatre Land complex in Deira, I have no information on any of

them. As none of the other developers has been in touch, I decide to take the initiative myself.

Lina is from Lebanon and started working on the Culture Metropolis three years ago. Billboards across the city, with artist's impressions of Persian-style wind-tower houses, promote the development to its pampered target clientele who presumably expect nothing less than the "Highly Sophisticated Arabian Lifestyle" on offer here. We're standing in the Culture Metropolis sales office, a marble hall the size of a tennis court, with the rear wall of glass etched with a vision of a future day in the life of Culture Metropolis, showing people in *dishdash*es and *abaya*s strolling among the villas and palm-lined avenues as children splash about with a dolphin and a jet soars over the skyline. This office could be a Sunni community centre, if there were such a thing. Though you might expect more people. We're alone here, apart from a sole Filipina eager to offer us a fruit juice.

Lina is about my age and you can tell by the deep, vertical furrows on the forehead of her rather stern visage that she doesn't have it easy here. She plays her cards close to her chest, as if she's unsure of how much she should or is allowed to say to me. Luckily there is an architect's model of Culture Metropolis on display in the middle of the foyer – on a plinth the size of a medium-sized swimming pool. The inevitable villas, office facilities and skyscrapers abound, all of them close to the Creek and of no particular distinction. Lina eyes me with Lebanese inscrutability and divulges that the masterplan has been approved, but that the details have yet to be filled in. There is no final, definitive model at present. That's fine; I'm more interested in the cultural buildings. Lena points to a structure resembling a warthog lounging in the sun. It had been designed as a museum of contemporary art. Had been? The complex next door, meanwhile, has been expanded to include a spa. "A pity," I say, and ask if there had been a development plan for this museum. Yes, Lina says, naming a gallery in London, and adding that no one has ever followed up on it.

I flip through the sales brochure and come across a young conductor in action with an orchestra. According to Lina, the location of the concert hall has not yet been confirmed. I take a closer look at the model. There isn't actually space for a concert hall on this luxury property rummage table. Lina attempts to dispel my misgivings. Things are still in flux. She can't say more at this stage. I am about to tell her that I think that's a shame, considering I am not a competitor but employed by a government agency to work with her on this and other projects, but she glances towards the lift where she spots someone she absolutely must introduce to me. Matthew casually shakes my hand and endures the introduction with eyes squeezed shut. He is barely five foot six and about fifty, with a rosy face and dark eyebrows that meet in the middle and which, on closer examination, appear to have been pencilled in. Matthew doesn't make eye contact, either when speaking or listening. He is Lina's boss and head planner of Culture Metropolis. He holds forth in a hoarse voice on rising sales figures and even greater pressure of deadlines, while I can't help thinking he wouldn't look out of place in a red-light district, with his skin-tight Versace suit and little leather

cap of the kind to be seen in shops selling S&M accessories. Matthew is Australian and burbles something about the Sydney Effect, or what Europeans might know as the Bilbao Effect – the idea that a single iconic, landmark building can transform the fortunes of an entire region. Culture Metropolis aims to emulate the Sydney Effect. But Matthew is evasive about the cultural buildings actually planned and the starchitects who will deliver them. It is, after all, still in flux. Apart from that, Matthew is short on time. His next client is waiting behind him – a Chinese and a reliable prospect for investment, probably. Lina's boss switches conversation partners seamlessly, so pressed for time he is unable to spare even a moment to say goodbye.

7 April
The Global Art World sales office features two caged panthers. The poor creatures pace back and forth, too distressed to dignify me with a glance. The pervasive smell of dead meat is curiously in keeping with the crocodile leather sofas and the deadbeat clients waiting in a

Ferrari in front of the door. Marie Louise is in charge of culture here. She's from Syria, she says, and launches straight into an explanation of the panthers, presumably out of embarrassment. Global Art World was originally conceived as a theme park with a strong emphasis on *The Jungle Book* – the Disney version, no doubt. Marie Louise has a pianist's fingers, from what I can see of them. Each hand sports an enormous gold ring studded with gems, covering all her digits but for her thumbs. In response to my questions, her bejewelled fingers flutter over palm groves, water features and villa developments in fruitless search of theatres and museums. It's a bit like a game of Monopoly. She's not allowed to show me the theme park itself, as currently conceived; it's currently under development by a Californian animation company.

So, all that remains is to inquire after Heritage Village. Interestingly, we have the devil's own job finding out where the manager for culture is based. The answer is nowhere, since no such person exists. The Village and its culture are in the hands of Hessam, a magistrate from the urban planning division. Hessam appears to have no proper office, so he elects to visit me. You can tell immediately that Hessam is no ordinary Emirati. In his late thirties and single, he lives modestly with his mother in a little house infelicitously located near the airport and directly under the flight path. Even Sheikh Mohammed had to acknowledge he had a point when Hessam asked why they had to build the airport so close to the city. He splutters this out barely before he's had the chance to remove a pile of papers from the chair to sit down. Hessam glances around at our chaos and declares it to be a nice place. "One should always work in pleasant surroundings," he opines, "or the fruits of one's labour are not worth the price." He changes the subject abruptly to talk of randomness and order. Chaos theory is his particular interest, he says; attempts to explain extreme fluctuations have met with so little success until recently. One might apply chaos theory to the Emirates, he muses. Unfortunately, he doesn't pursue this arresting notion and I realize that somehow in the course of his previous two sentences he's managed to switch to his wanderlust. His free time

takes him to Greenland and Patagonia, as he's particularly fond of glaciers – examples of extremes. And, while we're on the subject of climate, he declares that we should all take up cycling immediately.

Hessam may well be an environmentalist at heart, but he also has a lot to say about heritage. The Emiratis, he says, are not artistic and they hold their own traditions in disdain. It was the Indians who put them in Western clothes and the *dishdash* only came back into fashion when they decided to show the Indians and the rest of the world who calls the shots in this country. But culturally the Emiratis are bedouin, their origins hazy and their identity hard to pin down. If I want confirmation of this, all I need do is take a look at the traditional stick dance, he says. Don't the Masai dance like that? "Blessed are the dusty coasts behind Oman, who have acknowledged me without having seen me," recites Hessam. "That is what the Prophet is supposed to have said about this region. In other words, he didn't even have a name for the place."

So, what is to become of the Heritage Village, in the light of the Khor Dubai "announcement"? Hessam raises his hands, helplessly, his frazzled moustache quivering as he pouts like a defiant child. A theatrical gesture, proclaiming he has nothing to do with it and nor, emphatically, does he want anything to do with it. The things that appeal to him are Greenland, cycling and a beautiful, chaotic environment in which to work. What decidedly do not appeal are stress and new responsibilities.

9 April

The great and the good of the art market have set up shop in the city; it's trade fair time. Sheikh Mohammed opens the art fair attended by dozens of his so-called confidants including The Boss, Marwan, Salem and other Emirati colleagues of mine. I prefer to watch from the sidelines and turn up later than the others. One of the pieces on display has already caused a stir: a puppet of a camel peeking out from a footlocker. It evidently displeased not the ruler but some other influential establishment figure and is sentenced to disappear from view. The gallery responsible resists initially but concedes when the announcement is run on the news ticker. I anticipate accusations of art-market censorship in the British press and possibly in the French and German newspapers too. Even so, the usual suspects from Christie's, Sotheby's, New York's Chelsea District and London's Bond Street greet one another with florid air kisses at glamorous receptions, where artists like Ai Wei Wei, Daniel Buren and Tony Cragg are glad-handed and passed round with the canapés. The hectic pace of development, the skyscrapers and the cosmopolitan pzazz of this new 21st-century city are the hot topics on everyone's lips. They bear witness to the allure of new markets and celebrate the fast-selling contemporary art of Iran, pontificating about Dubai's future as an art market and offering hard financial analysis to news broadcasters reporting on a city they've experienced for just a day. No wonder they're all looking forward to sundowners on the beach, where the camel story provides the amusement of the day. I can't help feeling that honky-tonk puppet may be something of a Trojan camel portending doom for this ravenous industry.

Bouman is back and invites me to breakfast at the Grosvenor. It's as though we've known each other for years and that it's just the backdrop that has changed. He admits to a dearth of good architectural projects. We agree that this might have less to do with the market for architecture than with his own inclinations and, in an unexpected turn, he affirms that any project he undertook now would have to be of real interest personally to him. Bouman has to meet a client in fifteen minutes. Somehow during our hasty discussion we have pinpointed a vital aspect of culture, in the sense in which it emerges as an intrinsic part of urban planning. Is there any way of persuading Emiratis not to limit their consultations to the kind of experts who regard the importation of Perth or Miami as the last word in urban cultural sophistication? We talk about what Europe could contribute here – Europe as an exponent of cultural self-determination … culture as the natural expression of a society, the means by which it examines and constantly renews itself. We seem to have understood each other, at least. I have no museum to offer him, nor does Bouman seem to be angling for one.

I'm groping for ideas at first in our conversation, because I myself am not yet clear about the temporary space we might use to launch "Operation Culture": a multi-purpose venue suited to music, theatre and exhibitions, for Bharatanatyam dance, Arabic calligraphy, hip hop concerts and maybe even the Berlin Philharmonic; a centre for the arts that would be easy to build and wouldn't cost too much; in other words, a contradiction in every respect of the architectural reality of this city. "Ridiculously modest," says Bouman. It should be sited on the Creek, of course. I know of a disused amphitheatre-shaped site with a shaded view of the water, near the site allotted to our cultural complex, that we could convert for the purpose; a semicircle of wasteland between landscaped hummocks, forgotten amid the mêlée of construction sites, traffic jams and the endless streams of tourists headed for the souks.

10 April

Text messages bombard my mobile phone: "Enjoy off-peak rates on international calls" … "As of now, everything in Boulevard 1 is 70 percent off" … Galeano, Costume National and Serge Lutens all at sale prices … and Saks 5th Avenue is watching me, apparently. Where did all these people get my number? Perhaps it's Hessam's chaos theory in action.

You could argue that a shopping mall is merely a modern variation on the traditional Arab bazaar, technology making it possible for everyone, from prince to pauper, to shop in air-conditioned comfort in this insufferably hot desert climate. In the vast new Mall of the Emirates, technology goes one better than the usual glass lifts and escalators wafting customers from floor to marble, granite or porphyry floor, polished non-stop by Pakistani cleaners – there's a climate-controlled glass dome housing a ski slope complete with manufactured snow.

The anodyne warbling of piped muzak accompanies us browsers as we drift through the spotless galleries of designer boutiques. Stop

for a Grande Latte, handed over the counter by an Indonesian boy on minimum wage, and it just might occur to you to imagine the hands, the eyes, the thoughts of all the people across the world who have played a part in delivering the caffeine, water, milk and froth that you hold in that oversized paper cup. Then again, it might not.

Glance away, and you're likely to spot a typical Emirati family of four, the kids in *dishdash*es without the *ghutra*, swinging their arms to propel their lumbering bodies, too heavy and clumsy to romp and run like normal youngsters (obesity and diabetes in children are taking a heavy toll here), their slender mother a gliding figurine in black, hands at her chest clasping a pink mobile phone, her husband at her side, his chief function to brandish the credit card. But you're equally likely to see European tourists in shorts, with sunburned faces, scanning the shelves for bargains, or thirty-year-old Lebanese investment bankers slyly checking their reflections in shop windows,

affecting the gait of a model in a Boss ad, or British teens spilling out of the Cineplex having just seen Disney's *Ratatouille*, or Polish acrobats demonstrating their high-wire skills under the glass roof in the main atrium, or a French family pushing an overflowing supermarket trolley towards the car park, or clowns selling raffle tickets for a brand new Bentley, or real estate consultants hoping to tempt you with your dream villa in Culture Metropolis …

The shopping mall is a sadomasochistic funhouse of global consumerism. It far transcends the simple old-fashioned business of exchanging cash for essential goods. It's consumer porn, an interminable transacting of stimulated desire and temporary relief; lust after the brand and suffer the exquisite whiplash of the price tag – of the new waisted *abaya* from Dior, the Louis Vuitton purse with the unusual silver clasp and 12-carat rock, the silk carpet from Isfahan and the to-die-for olive bread from Paul (fondée en 1889), the designer sunglasses and garlic presses, that exclusive luggage or the eye-wateringly priced Ming vase. And for the lads, well, there

are the Lego Bionicles and the Game Boys to tantalize and excite the compulsive drive for relief, a tame simulacrum of the testosterone-fuelled release found on the football terraces or in street fights elsewhere.

A "Classic Wave" millennium edition stretch limousine pulls up outside the Mall's Kempinski Hotel and disgorges about fifteen seven- or eight-year-olds on their way to a birthday party at the St Moritz Café, right by the ski slope. But they don't seem particularly excited. Some of the youngsters drag themselves along, grappling with large gift-wrapped presents; others have their nannies do the carrying for them. Their mothers escort them, leaving their Cayennes and Landcruisers to the valet parking. They are expats from Britain and France and Saudis or Emiratis in Western dress, arms loaded with bracelets, glossy hair pulled back in bandeaus, skin lightly tanned, elegant and passionately focused on their offspring.

You watch them go, strangely alive to the aura of this gentle avarice, enveloped as you are by the scent of candyfloss, incense,

Chanel No. 5 and Nappa leather – perspiration is for mere mortals. The birthday party must be well under way by now but you remain rooted to the polished marble spot, frozen by the siren call of Mammon's massed choirs in your ears, singing of eternal desire, luring you with the promise of endless happiness. How can you resist?

11 April

A second breakfast with Bouman in the Grosvenor. His assistants have sent the drawings in advance – an amphitheatre and art gallery, a box-like structure for mounting temporary exhibitions. It reminds me of the Mies van der Rohe New National Gallery building in Berlin with its square, glass exhibition space and flat, cantilevered roof from which a curtain can be hung to shield the amphitheatre from the elements. The gallery has – as I had hoped – a portable annex, which can be moved down the Creek or dismantled, transported and reassembled elsewhere. The estimated cost is about 30 million dollars and completion time will be approximately twelve months. I say it is reminiscent of a pavilion. Bouman beams.

Salem offers no opinion when I present the idea. I call a meeting with the others that morning to see what they make of the "Creek Pavilion for Theatre and Art" (my working title). They like it, not least because a famous architect has designed it. They have, in fact, never heard of Bouman, but Khalil googles him and they are impressed. Salem drops by in the afternoon with good news. The Boss has given the project his general approval. But before we can formally present the plan we must check its feasibility.

So I contact companies specializing in construction project management and meet three candidates that same day. They have all won fat contracts for the usual hotel/office/shopping monstrosities proliferating here and they all tell me the same thing. Our Pavilion is too small. It won't be easy to interest anyone in pitching for our modest project. One, an Australian who reminds me of the craggy, desert wanderer Travis in the film *Paris, Texas*, lectures me in a thin and weary voice. "There's too much going on here for anyone to be bothered with a trifling project like this, with all its complications," he says. "Planning offices and development companies won't even listen unless the contract is worth more than a billion dirhams. You're talking peanuts here," he says, softening. "It'll only fly if the ruler personally requests that somebody do it." I get the message and promise to touch base with him again.

13 April

My neighbours are having a fight; their voices are interfering with my dreamland conversation with Bouman about the Pavilion. Now someone's wailing. I start from my sleep and the commotion outside resolves itself into not only voices, but the wailing of an alarm. Blearily dragging myself to my feet, I feel my way around the apartment without switching on the light. The wailing grows more insistent. It's not coming from the neighbour's apartment, but from my own kitchen. No, not the kitchen, it's everywhere! The siren drills down into my cerebellum. I grab the shirt and trousers draped over my chair, look helplessly around and feel about for my briefcase, the pulse in my neck throbbing and my legs heavy. Outside in the hallway, doors stand ajar. The alarm is now so loud it brings tears to the eyes. The lifts are out of order and eventually I find the door to the fire escape stairs. The distance from landing to landing is only seven steps and I take them in a single bound. I'm reminded of how, as a seven-year-old on my way to school, I ambitiously attempted more and more steps until I could whiz down a whole flight in the high-rise where I lived with my parents.

But this time I'm panicked with fear and feel as if I'm flying in slow motion, before a dead end stops me in my tracks on the 33rd floor. I find a fire door at the other end of the hall, which I open by depressing a horizontal bar, and find another yawning stairwell ahead. There are crates obstructing my way one floor down, bags full of rubbish to negotiate and, farther down still, a bicycle directly blocking the stairway. I catch sight of someone in the shadows just below me and in a single jump I'm right behind him. It's Khalil, my corpulent Bahraini neighbour, who mutters and wobbles his Falstaffian way down the stairs. Khalil is the only other competitor in this race for survival and he has no choice but to take each step one at a time. I pull up short and, the wailing torture of the siren notwithstanding, gulp down a deep draught of air. I link arms with him down the last few flights and some minutes later – though it feels like an age – we find ourselves face-to-face with an Indian security guard who has materialized from one of the corridors and stares at us, bewildered. He seems clueless as to what's going on and is unable to tell us where we should go. So, we go it alone and pursue a few blind alleys before finally finding the ground-floor reception area. Strangely, the residents of the building are all panicking here rather than gathered outside. Several young oriental women are cowering on the matching suite of sofas and chairs, whimpering. One or two Arabs are berating the uniformed Indians by the lifts. And, in a bizarre echo of *Dad's Army*, someone hollers in German, "Keine Panik!"

The doors slide open and an ebony-skinned, middle-aged man enters wearing a white skullcap, followed by an Emirati chauffeur carrying his suitcase behind him. The black man has great flared nostrils that lend his face a haughty expression, as though he regards all of us here as behaving like sissies. I'm grateful for all the shrieking, as it helps to drown out the sound of the siren. Khalil, the only man in a *dishdash*, pushes his way to the reception desk and buttonholes the weedy fellow behind the counter, who responds with an upward jerk of his bony shoulders as if it were he who was being accused of arson. The clock above his head shows it's half two.

Ten minutes later, someone manages at last to kill the siren. Calm is gradually restored and the residents drift back to their apartments. Khalil comes up to me with a dismissive shrug. Someone had been smoking in the stairwell and triggered the alarm. The security staff didn't know how to shut it off and someone had to go for help. Stepping into the lift with him I feel my left leg buckle beneath me. I can no longer feel the backs of my knees.

15 April

Aching muscles, probably due as much to panic-attack cramps as my antics on the stairs, have condemned me to immobility yesterday and today, so I have been holding the fort at my computer in my apartment. The familiar lights of the towers and construction sites keep up their constant twinkling outside, but somehow my position here suddenly seems less assured today than it did before.

16 April

Aida on Fire in the garden of the Abu Dhabi Emirates Palace Hotel affords a good opportunity to sit back and observe the culture on offer here. It's a three-and-a-half-hour German production with fireworks, on tour through twenty countries in Asia and South America. The orchestra and choir are from Ústí nad Labem in the Czech Republic and the singers are unlikely to have graced the programme of any reputable opera house. I sit in the makeshift theatre space under open skies adjacent to the beach, surrounded by tents, listening to music that sounds like a phonograph recorded in the middle of a 1945 bombing raid in Germany. The hissing and crackling from the electric amplifier is augmented by a buffeting wind blowing in from the Gulf. Aida, Radames and Amneris stand facing one another, attempting to elicit an emotional response with the odd gesture of passion, but the disturbance is embarrassing for them too, of course. Palm trees sway behind me and a half-moon rises over the floodlights. The fireworks are cancelled on account of the breeze. I am sitting in the area reserved for artistes' guests. Two Russian couples to my left have stashed champagne in the gardens, which explains why they slip out now and again, coming back in ever more jovial spirits. Eventually they go too far for an Arab in front of them. The man spits behind him with the subtlety of a seasoned opera-goer from bourgeois Berlin and a hush settles for a few moments. The American couple to my right keep talking. He can't make out the surtitles and she wants to know what language exactly the people up there are singing in. Sitting in front of us in the "diamond stalls", next to the assorted Highnesses and Excellencies are the people who call this place home: women in dark, elegant veils and men in white *dishdash*es. They absorb the exotic spectacle among the pyramids on stage with rapt attention and find no cause to duck out into the gardens. When the performance ends, their applause is the most enthusiastic in the audience.

During the intermission I retreat to one of the giant pillow seats by the water and smoke a *sheesha*. The Emirates Palace squats behind a palm grove like a fat glow-worm in the sand. Its cupola changes colour every twenty seconds. Emotionally I feel most in tune with the green. When the show is over I wait at the hotel entrance for fifteen minutes for a taxi to take me back. Fourteen Porsches, eight Bentleys and five Ferraris drive up as I wait. On the return trip through the desert night I ask the driver to switch on the radio. We find a station with some nice Mumbai pop and I slump back in my seat with relief.

21 April

The address is Kensington, not far from Imperial College. Salem is sitting next to me in the minivan that collected us from the hotel, watching in silence as we drive by the cyclists and roller skaters beneath the fluffy green trees of Hyde Park. I don't know if The Boss has told him more about this meeting than he's letting on, but I'm still pretty much in the dark. Salem is in jeans and turtleneck and it's the first time I've seen him in Western dress – he confessed at the airport that he feels uncomfortable not wearing his *dishdash*. He has clearly attempted to brush his black hair but it's standing up every which way as if in protest at the new dress code which he feels he must now adopt. The car draws into a private road and passes through the raised barrier. We stop in front of a wrought-iron gate. Salem taps a code into the keypad and the gate glides open. The townhouses here are Victorian, though you wouldn't guess their age from looking at them. We step into a hallway and take the lift upstairs where a young man is waiting for us, in a black suit, the jacket stretched taught across his muscular shoulders. He nods curtly and walks a few steps ahead, with a wrestler's gait, before opening a swing door to a spacious office suite. An Arab approaches whom I recognize as one of the men with the Sheikh when we met a few weeks ago in the Emirates Tower Hotel lobby. He seems affable, gives a firm handshake, and leads us to the salon where Sheikh Mansour and another man are seated on the Le Corbusier sofa, conferring hastily and in hushed tones, as though there's some business they're just finishing up. On our approach the Sheikh calls out a salutation, first in Arabic and then in English, and the gentlemen rise to take a seat with us nearer the fireplace at an antique walnut table, strewn with art catalogues and modern calligraphic artwork. An Asian housekeeper scurries in and takes drinks orders. Sheikh Mansour is wearing a light, tailored suit distinguished by brown leather lapels, and a super-skinny, charcoal tie with his cream shirt. His sparse hair is cut short, lending him an ascetic look, but the way in which he gets straight down to business seems slightly out of character to me. I know he's the type who loves to gossip, and I detect something a little camp lurking behind his façade of seriousness – for example in the way he flourishes his manicured hands to admire his fingernails.

With a casual yet graceful movement of his hand he introduces Mr Matthieu, a marketing luminary and sometime art dealer with offices in Paris, Geneva and London. Mr Matthieu, by his own admission, speaks Arabic very badly despite having an Algerian mother, and is an art lover who's made a pile of money it seems from arranging the large-scale entertainment events for which he's famed: Formula 1 parties, the Fashion Week events in Paris, Miami and New York, the G8 summit receptions, and the Cannes Film Festival awards ceremony. He's probably in his mid-fifties and, according to Sheikh Mansour, knows everyone worth knowing in the world of politics, economics and culture. Matthieu listens to all this with feigned indifference and adds that his true loves are primarily the arts and sport. In that order.

With Sheikh Mansour and Matthieu presumably knowing at least as much as we do about our "mission", there's no need to beat about the bush. The Sheikh gets straight to the point. The objective of our meeting is to determine the key steps in developing a strategy that will enable the Cultural Council to do its work. He and I have already had discussions to this end. At this point the assistant sitting next to him eagerly hands him a piece of paper which His Highness treats with lofty disregard and pays no further attention to.

He has already spoken with The Boss about his design centre project and has received approval. The architect Zold is, according to Sheikh Mansour, a rising star on the European scene. I have never heard of him myself, but I don't let on. I assume from the name that he's Hungarian. Sheikh Mansour tells me that Zold has been informed and is available at any time for detailed discussions, and that his own company is currently in discussion with one of the world's top design schools. Sheikh Mansour also plans to establish a film school with a renowned Californian partner. And as for Mr Matthieu ... well, his experience of events planning and marketing will be invaluable.

Matthieu butts in just as the Sheikh is in full flow and explains to Salem that his company has previously been involved with several large projects in the Middle East, including international cultural festivals at Baalbek and Byblos, and concerts featuring Madonna and the Stones some years ago in Giza. Plans are in the offing for a local office in Dubai.

Matthieu is happily getting into his stride when he in turn is interrupted by a short man with wispy white hair who breezes in. I recognize him immediately as Banderas, the bestselling French-Argentinian novelist with a mystical tendency and a penchant for female lonely hearts. He's sporting black jeans and a black sweater but above all an ingratiating grin, his full lips giving him the licentious air of a satyr. He struts about as he makes his way towards us, declaiming in his turbocharged, staccato Hispanic English a loud parody of complaint to Sheikh Mansour about not being let past the gate, pausing histrionically and checking each corner of the salon, and generally making an entrance worthy of a Comédie-Française production of *Tartuffe*. Sheikh Mansour pays lip service to these remonstrations and reels off something about the erratic behaviour of British security guards. He briefly introduces Banderas to … whom, I wonder? Salem appears already to have known about his participation in this meeting and I suspect Banderas very probably had a meeting with The Boss some time ago. The Sheikh summarizes our "discussion" thus far, and as I listen to him it is borne in on me that when he makes a pronouncement, the matter, as far as he is concerned, is as good as discussed.

But then our writer takes the floor. He scratches his short, close-trimmed beard and in an oracular, confidential tone, as if he were imparting state secrets, paints two possible scenarios for the future of the Middle East. "Either everything is going to go up in smoke in an Arab-Israeli-Iranian-American conflict," he predicts, "or the successful young cities of the Gulf will become the new models for peace and beneficial interaction with the world." I notice Sheikh Mansour and Matthieu lean back and exchange a quick glance. They seem favourably disposed and I would guess this is not the first time they have heard Banderas talk this way. "The world is at home in this new city on the Gulf," the writer continues, almost in a whisper. He's getting so many inquiries from the region, he claims, that he's had to produce an Arabic version of his website, much to his designer's irritation. His latest book (set in Dubai) has notched up phenomenal sales across the Muslim world. "The city is a *role model* for modern Islam," he says, "but also for Christianity too, because nowhere else will you find this kind of tolerant equality between individuals of opposing faiths. The only thing missing," he concludes, tucking his feet under him so he's cross-legged on the chair in Buddha pose, "is … *soul*." Banderas pauses for effect, before asking me: "Which cities, in your opinion, should be our *role models* for cultural development?" Entering into the spirit of the performance, I take my time, looking round the circle at each of them, sensing possible boredom on Matthieu's part, at least. "Berlin and Barcelona," I declare at last, testing my audience. Banderas struggles to his feet from his cross-legged position, circumambulates the table, and wrings my hand.

"Correct!" he cries, "My opinion exactly!" He is ecstatic, but none the less sincere for that.

I peer over at Sheikh Mansour who also seems satisfied. Banderas resumes his Buddha pose on the chair. The moment has come to express my thanks for such encouraging support and from such illustrious patrons, which I do with a gracious smile. Banderas scratches his beard again. Of course, what is needed is for someone to set up a world council for global culture with its headquarters in Dubai. In fact, he would even volunteer himself as an ambassador for such an organization.

As we bowl back through Hyde Park in the minivan, Salem offers his first significant comment of the day: "Matthieu will have to be on board," he says. "There can be no culture without events. Large concerts, big fairs, festivals. Matthieu can do that. And Banderas. Banderas is His Highness's friend." And, Salem avers, the city needs friends like him and Sheikh Mansour. "Friends who will replace our projects with their own businesses?" Salem stares straight ahead over the driver's shoulder. Those decisions are not his to make, he says. "And that's not an answer," I object, making it clear I certainly wouldn't want to work under such conditions. Salem takes it all in his stride. He says he's grateful for my openness, which is why, after all, I am Mr Culture. The government will still have to think it all through and, anyway, any concerns I may have in that regard should be mitigated by the fact that no one has questioned the Deira complex to date. If only I were to trust in the current management structure just a little, then I'd see. It might at least be a comfort to know that they are currently looking for a Director General for the Cultural Council.

We're with Touitou, our architect, in the afternoon, at his studio in Islington. He's a chain-smoking, gangly guy with a grey mane in his late fifties and is uneasy that the construction contract has not yet been signed. I tell him that I was not aware of that and he gives me his version of events: Marwan summoned him to the city two years ago and broke the news that they wanted to build his design. He was asked to stay on for another day and next morning was called to some ballroom, where he met the ruler in the company of a few dozen Emiratis and local media. They all sat at a long table with an architect's model of his design in front of them. The ruler congratulated him live on camera. Marwan escorted him from the hall later, assuring him the project development phase would be set in motion immediately and that he would be in touch. The following day, the press reported that the ruler had announced the building of the largest theatre complex in the Arab world. There was a photo of Touitou and his model with His Highness. The article made much of Touitou's Yemeni roots, the inference being that Arabs are great architects by tradition. Then months went by before he and Marwan were in touch again. Azad calls occasionally, but his impression is that, so far, nothing much is happening.

Salem is disgruntled at hearing all this. I am not sure whether it's Touitou's whinging that has rubbed him up the wrong way, or the fact that he spoke at all.

23 April

After the sleepless overnight flight back to Dubai, it's another day in the familiar chaos of office life – chaotic even though Latifa and the others are off on a course "Discovering the Elite Within" themselves. It makes little difference if Carmen, Salem (who spends most of his time on the 52nd floor anyway) and I have the place to ourselves; it's still like Grand Central Station in here. We're now receiving about two hundred and fifty emails a day, at least half of which are in languages other than English.

The heat chokes me, even on the short evening walk from one air-conditioned zone to the next, from the lift to the car park. It's not just the high temperature that's debilitating but the greasy, saturating humidity, for which one would like to blame our proximity to the Gulf but which carries the faint smell of effluent.

My turtles are no longer the same size as each other. Just three days out of my sight and already something fishy is going on. Are they really two females? I take them out of the water and weigh them in my hands. Yes, a considerable difference in weight. The bigger one shoves the little one aside while feeding and only lets it in when it's had enough. Why didn't I notice this before? At least there's one tangible outcome from my trip to London.

The heavy breath of night steams up the windows. The tower under construction next to my apartment has almost reached eye level. Floodlights pick out the workers among the intricate nexus of scaffolding poles, wooden planks and concrete walls they've erected. The men are less than a hundred yards across from me. They wear white helmets, which in daylight render their dark faces shadowy and indistinguishable. I see them occasionally by the multi-storey car park behind my apartment building, leaning against the wooden fence as they wait for the bus to take them back to their labour camps. Most of them are around twenty and speak little or no English. Their homeland of Kerala in India is just a three-hour flight from here. They regard you with shock and amazement if you stop the car to speak, but they're happy to make contact. One of them once gave me his cellphone number and showed me a Polaroid picture of his father, a man of indefinable age with an emaciated face and thin sideburns.

Travel by boat on the backwaters of Kerala along the Malabar coast and you'll find yourself in a shimmering labyrinth of waterways, lakes and canals, fed by the monsoon rains, fringed with tropical palms and reed beds, which fishermen and merchants navigated centuries ago and where stilt-legged birds wait motionless for frogs. Between Kuttanad and Alappuzha it's like the set of a watery South Indian road movie, with its Christian churches, boys in skullcaps playing cricket in the courtyards, women pounding and hauling their laundry in the dark brackish waters, fishermen setting their nets for the night, and white tourists buying one-dollar *abaya*s they'll never wear from waterside stalls. This is what it means to live below the poverty line. The villages, built precariously on levees no more than

a water-scoop's reach above the surface, are home to the very same hovels from which Dubai's construction workers hail. Their shacks are so close to the waterline as to offer little or no protection from flooding, lending the term "skid row" an even grimmer and more literal meaning.

The half-built towers beyond my window are transformed by night into a multiplex doll's house of a myriad room-sized sets, each a scene in the untold, unfolding drama of Dubai's anonymous construction workers, stage lighting supplied by a neon strip light hanging from the ceiling of the unglazed concrete cubicle. The pious man is at his prayers, kneeling, standing, prostrating himself in endless spiritual exercise before a wall he probably constructed himself until, exhausted and resigned, he squats in a corner, his back to me. A brawl breaks out on the floors above, the crane operator shining a spotlight on the action. Three workers hold a man aloft as another lays into him, punching him repeatedly. Others come running and drag the beaten man into a niche away from the beam of light. Someone waves the crane operator over, to take the injured man down to ground level, presumably. The scene is so fleeting I am unable completely to grasp what's going on but it puts me in mind of Hugo von Hofmannsthal's famous poem, *Manche Freilich*: "Granted, some must die below the deck, Where creak the vessel's heavy oars. Others live above at the open helm, Knowing flights of birds and realms of stars." Except, here in Dubai, they're dying high above ground level as well.

24 April

I take my young wards back to the salesperson in the Crown Plaza mall. He can't be sure they're the same sex after all; it's possible the smaller turtle is male. Should I be expecting offspring, I wonder? Is there such a thing as contraception? The man is a Muslim from Tehran. He is disinclined to answer such questions.

26 April

A reunion with Yusuf the *badawi*. He calls me mid-morning and wants to know if I'm free. We meet up outside the Audi showroom on Sheikh Zayed Road. He is dressed exactly the same as he was when I first met him, grabs my thumb while shaking hands as if to demonstrate a special intimacy between us, and chauffeurs us in the Toyota pickup I recall from my desert sojourn, up and over the highway to the camel racetrack and stables at Nad Al Sheba. Saturday is the busy day here. Men swarm in from desert and suburbs in their white Landcruisers and quad bikes to tend to their animals. Beyond the camel stalls is a parking area with space for a few thousand vehicles, designed for bigger meetings than the one today, surely. Official races are no longer run with child jockeys bought from poor Pakistani families – they have been replaced by robots – though Yusuf assures me that in the desert, away from the official tracks, they still use human jockeys as they always have. He admits the unofficial racecourses in the desert are no good, but he thinks the little robots in their racing silks are silly.

The Pakistani grooms have a lot to do on Saturdays if the owners are to get their money's worth. Everyone wants his camel to be judged worthy of exhibition in the enclosure. The grooms look down the camels' muzzles, pull back their eyelids, lift their tails, and pat all the way down the neck and abdominal wall until the animals start to belch.

An official bellows orders at the grooms who command their animals to stand, turn, and kneel – a touch of the camel-stick helps. Men stand chattering and smoking together, enveloped by dust, fussing over their own animals and inspecting the others. The noise swells and ebbs and swells again, in rhythm with the mood of the proceedings. The camels take it all in their stride, with a sidelong glance and a slow bat of a stoical eyelid. They neither resist the commands of owners and grooms, nor are they in any hurry to comply. Their ambling gait lends them a serenity you don't see in other ungulates. They make walking seem *cool*. They are somehow redolent of civil servants in the impression they give of secure and measured lives. Now and then, one of the bedouin mounts a camel, pulls tight on the rein, and clicks his tongue until the animal raises itself off its haunches and condescends to walk in a circle. At a certain point, both camel and rider tire of going round and round and take off, past the Landcruisers, across the flat, open country and the six-lane highway to Oman, and into the desert proper, on a little tour through the dunes.

I stand apart from the crowd until they bring Yusuf's dromedaries out of the stall. It turns out he owns only seventeen animals, a good deal fewer than the other owners. He beckons me over and shows me his favourite female. The animal is small, not yet two years old, Yusuf says – a teenager in human years. He shows me her teeth, shiny light brown stones in a little dark red cave. I discover a yawning cavity between the canine and molars. Yusuf assures me this is normal in camels and prises open the mouths of two other animals to demonstrate. He lets me mount an older male and leads the way on another. We do a lap around the parking lot and past the stalls to the racetrack. But the riders are crowding one another, and my mount gets a little nervous and wants to pass Yusuf, despite his talking to calm him down. So we return to the pen where the herd eyes us, nonchalantly.

Yusuf insists on escorting me back into town even though he usually spends the entire day here on a Saturday. Before jumping into my car back at the Audi showroom, I invite him out for a *sheesha*. He hesitates but accepts when I suggest a café he knows and where locals mingle. I pick up a publication off the front passenger seat as Yusuf climbs in. It's a catalogue for an exhibition suggested by a small museum in Freiburg, Germany: the earliest photographs of bedouin in existence, taken by a Dutchman and an Egyptian between 1860 and 1890. Flipping through the booklet for a moment I gaze at the faces, parched by the sun and abraded by sand. There are men in thobes, young girls like statues in bridal dresses, a barber with his razor, a man on a horse, an old woman in a *niqab* at a well, surrounded by children. The exhibition is entitled *Muslim Faces*. I have an idea and, while we're puffing on our *sheesha* pipes, show the catalogue to Yusuf. He turns the pages slowly, chuckling to himself now and again. Then he becomes serious and says that people dressed strangely in those days, but that some of them look like his mother's parents and his cousins in Saudi Arabia. I tell him these photos are old and very valuable. He asks where I got the book and I tell him the pictures belong to a collector in Switzerland. Yusuf can't understand why someone in Switzerland should be interested in such pictures, but he's happy about it. "If nobody had collected these pictures," he says, "then they wouldn't exist anymore and no one would know how the people looked back then."

28 April

Phoned Frau Sturzenegger, the curator of the Gysin Collection in Freiburg. So I received the catalogue, did I? And the promptness of my response! Just as one would expect from the fastest city on Earth! Judging by her accent Frau Sturzenegger is from Switzerland and imagines we already have a full programme of exhibitions, with whole armies of curators and support staff. Ah, if only. In which museum complex were you hoping to show, dear Frau Sturzenegger? We might manage the little ballroom at the Fairmont Hotel or the large one in Madinat Jumeirah. Heck, if we really push the boat out we might even be able to reserve you a corner of the fast food strip at the International Finance Centre. Frau Sturzenegger reveals that the photographs have already been shown in Uzbekistan and the collector, based in Zug in Switzerland, is keen to mount an exhibition with us. The Saudi royal family had offered him several million dollars for the photos three years ago, but he wanted to hang on to them so he could exhibit them all over the Muslim world. Impressive. There's seems to be no ulterior motive behind this proposal than a sincere ambition to show objects of art where they belong. Why not have 19th-century photographs of Muslims to open the cultural programme of a city where no such thing had been done before …? Yusuf! If it hadn't been for him, I might never have thought of it.

There'd be no need for a last-minute round-up of Picassos and Rembrandts. The autumn programme could kick off with *Muslim Faces*. We have a presentation with The Boss the day after tomorrow. By that time, Salem, Khalil and I will have determined whether there's any alternative to holding the exhibition in a 5-star tourist pleasure dome.

The German consul-general calls later that day. He's already heard from Frau Sturzenegger. Ah, the marvels of diplomacy! A good project, I say, albeit from Germany.

29 April

Latifa is in the office at eight for the first time ever. The others arrive a few minutes later, in high spirits despite the early start. As far as I can tell, they are recounting stories of their brothers and brothers-in-law. The male sex is an endless source of amusement, regardless of whether their male colleagues are about, as they are today. The reason for this uncharacteristic promptness is our appearance before The Boss tomorrow. Salem has given everyone a project or topic for which they must prepare PowerPoint slides. I am included in this meeting but feel as though I'm looking at the whole thing from the outside, curious but perplexed. I suppose this is the way they make strategy decisions at Credit Suisse and General Motors, too. Perhaps that's why so much has gone awry. How do you give a top manager the impression he has understood it all to the point he has the confidence to give the thing his blessing, when of course he doesn't understand or couldn't be expected to? Well, you have to keep him entertained for a start and do absolutely nothing to undermine his confidence in any way. Salem asks us nicely to communicate in graphics and buzzwords rather than blocks of indigestible infor-mation, and to describe highly complex technical or contextual interrelations, spanning fiscal years and representing billions in investment, in a cartoon form that recalls the golden age of Hollywood animation and Daffy Duck creator Tex Avery. And it has to look perfect, be totally slick and betray no trace of ambiguity. One hundred percent affirmation. Any risk or downside is to be addressed verbally and only if absolutely necessary – unless the aim is to kill the project off entirely.

I try to imagine how it would be if opera directors had to present their creative ideas by means of business-friendly PowerPoint shows. First the vision: Don Giovanni (with a picture of Mount Everest). The mission: Mozart as global market leader for the opera. Strategy: an ultra-contemporary interpretation of the piece, of course. Action plan: to be determined at the first rehearsal. Then slides of set and costume designs. Add a few bars of music. What a pity I'm not "implementing" that kind of project myself any longer …

On the subject of music, our presentation team turns out to be somewhat challenged in the imagination department. My young colleagues do actually know something about design but setting their images to a musical soundtrack proves tricky. I contribute with a few titles on my iPod sent to me by a baritone from Amsterdam – accompanied of course by his urgings to stage a performance in the very near future. There's a fairly imaginative improvisation on the *darbuka*, a goblet-shaped drum used in Islamic music, which accompanies the Dutch singer's genuinely heart-rending ballad. Khalil has already downloaded it and synchronized it with the slides when he discovers it's the work of an exiled Iraqi group that's banned here because of its links with a well-known (though, of course, repressed) homosexual movement active in the Islamic world. That leaves us with the lounge music CD of a hotel chain run by a government-owned holding company. At least that should be harmless enough.

At about midnight, after sixteen hours' solid work, we run through the presentation on Salem's computer. Yes, it works! He sends the document to The Boss's office, so they can see it in advance of tomorrow's meeting. Just to be on the safe side.

5

1 May

Yesterday's meeting with The Boss was postponed until today – Labour Day, which has no resonance here, of course, but surely can't be a bad omen. We're presenting in the conference room on the 52nd floor. Salem doesn't seem to know until the last minute who will be there. At reception we learn that the party will include not only Sheikh Mansour and Matthieu but also our President, His Highness Sheikh Majed bin Mohammed Al Maktoum. There is an air of Christmassy expectation. Mansour, Matthieu and The Boss emerge from the adjoining room, The Boss cranking up his volume. Mansour has a preoccupied air and vouchsafes no more than a brief hello. Matthieu, however, is already chattering away with Latifa and Mona and seems cock-a-hoop. The meeting actually starts more or less on time though The Boss dashes out suddenly, to meet His Highness and escort him to the conference room. The young prince enters – with The Boss in his wake, sporting a huge grin – and everyone rises and returns his Arabic greeting. He then takes a seat on one of the two chairs at the head of the diamond-shaped table and shoots a glance of special curiosity at me.

His Highness is a little stiff and awkward and seems at a loss what to do with his hands. His delivery is halting and his voice hoarse, as though he's suffering from a cold. He blinks into space without meeting anyone's eye, his face seeming to mirror the uncertainty of

his audience. He opens his speech – thankfully in English – with his father's vision for the city, and expresses his pride in being associated with the Cultural Council. He has great expectations of us. "When I am as old as you are," he says to me, "I might also be an opera director." Cue sycophantic titters all round, while Mansour contorts his features into an oleaginous smirk that persists for the duration of the meeting. We then let our multimedia presentation roll for the next seventy minutes, the in-house lounge music soundtrack tinkling vacuously away. There are a few questions from Mansour, The Boss – principally in relation to the museums strategy – and even Sheikh Majed, but we only get about two-thirds of the way through the show. Salem has a ready explanation for skipping part of it and focusing only on the essentials. My main concern had been that someone would find fault with our suggestion of just two museums when the Khor Dubai announcement had made provision for seventy-two institutions. I needn't have worried. The idea of a World Museum, involving the participation of international partners and deals with global culture, is met with universal approval. Even the

Pavilion passes muster. The Boss is unsure, however, whether the amphitheatre site I had in mind is the right place for it.

Sheikh Majed turns sharply, peers at us uncertainly from under his *ghutra* and nods at The Boss. In two short sentences he thanks us in English for the presentation, without commenting on it, then mumbles something in Arabic that the Emiratis and Mansour receive with various degrees of enthusiasm. I am given to understand that protocol does not allow for any discussion with him. Presumably he and The Boss will share their opinions in private. We leave the room with Sheikh Majed and exchange our farewells at reception. Before stepping into the lift, he turns to me and says: "The Pavilion is a very good idea. We should focus our efforts on that."

The Boss accompanies Sheikh Majed downstairs and does not return. Instead, he sends his office manager Behula to tell us he will let us know through Salem how things are to proceed. I enquire whether we should in any event go ahead with "Muslim Faces". Khalil has come up with a viable plan for exhibiting the photos at the International Finance Centre after the summer. Everyone stands around stumped for a moment until Behula answers that it would be best to hold it during Ramadan. I'm not clear on what authority she speaks but want to know if we can now start getting in touch with international museums. She confers briefly with Salem, querying the role of international museums in all this, then nods. "Just keep working on it," she says, with a laugh that could mean anything. Salem stays behind on the 52nd floor. I expect they're having a debriefing.

4 May

Salem brings no clear brief from the 52nd floor. I recall The Boss exclaiming: "That's how we're going to do it!" twice during the presentation. But are we really going to do it? It seems to me decisions are made in stages. There is *approval*, *final approval* and *final, final approval*. Initial *approval* is not enough. All we know for sure at the moment is that we can start preparing *Muslim Faces*. I ask

Frau Sturzenegger to provide costs. The amount (including provision for a catalogue) doesn't seem very substantial to me. I tell her so and ask her to take into account the fact that everything will probably have to be imported, including workers to handle installation.

It hadn't occurred to Salem that showing a hundred old photos might cost so much. He is visibly shocked. I tell him we would have to shell out four times that amount for paintings by old and so-called new masters. Assuming we could get them at all. This news sets him ruminating even more. Asked for the third time this afternoon if we have approval for the Pavilion, he says "No". And then he drops his bombshell: "The financing for the whole project is still up in the air." I ask him what he means exactly by "the whole project". "Culture," comes the reply.

10 May

Abdul-Hamid from the Sailing House shyly poked his head in yesterday. He was actually looking for Salem, hoping to muster support against the Municipality in its suit against him in respect of the illegal addition built to store Hassan's early work. He has a gentle nature but I can see he's furious. "What's the point of the Khor Dubai development and the Cultural Council, if artists are treated like criminals?" he fumes. "All this talk of a new local arts scene is no more than business as usual. It's the profit to be made from over-hyped Iranian artists that interests galleries. Emiratis are left to fall by the wayside."

He's probably right, there's not much homegrown talent in evidence, apart from the occasional piece by a young Emirati in a local photo exhibition. Abdul-Hamid is long gone when it dawns on me that the thing to do is to get Hassan's work exhibited internationally. Then, perhaps, they might take more notice of the talent at home. For want of a better idea I email Frau Sturzenegger and ask if she knows of a gallery in Europe that might be willing, at short notice, to show Emirati art. It wouldn't be a commercial thing but more an attempt to turn the tables and export culture rather than import it, for a change.

Frau Sturzenegger responds right away. This very summer, at the beginning of July in fact, there's an opportunity to mount a small exhibition at the Gysin Collection. It would be a very welcome complement to *Muslim Faces*. I am to feel free to take her email as an invitation.

11 May

The Sailing House is already working on a budget. Fortuitously they have a useful visitor: Piet, a long-haired Dutchman of indeterminate age whose emaciated, furrowed and unnaturally ruddy face, not to mention his near-toothless mouth, recalls the late Chet Baker. Not only is Piet an old friend of Hassan's but he was also the organizer (he doesn't like the word curator) of his first exhibition three years ago in Arnhem. Which explains why Piet knows a lot about logistics and costs. In the space of just two hours he has already worked out an exhibition proposal for sixty paintings, drawings, photos and objects by five Emirati artists connected with the Sailing House. Salem doesn't quite know what to make of the whole thing but, emboldened by Latifa, he determines to approach The Boss about the budget. Latifa has proved herself a galvanizing force time and again. Today she announces that she will collect money from her own family if the government can't sort it out. At this, Salem smiles and says it would be a welcome initiative, though the government would have to give its approval first.

Which The Boss has seen to, apparently – after indirect intervention by Latifa (via her influential Papa, I suspect). Beaming, she tells me that we now have a two-hundred-thousand euro deficit guarantee for the first public and official government-sponsored exhibition of Emirati art abroad. The opening is set for 12 July. Piet will travel to meet Frau Sturzenegger in three days to talk about the logistics. They've already come up with a title for the show: *Dubai Now*.

12 May

Azad admits there has been no activity in the way of culture at Al Adheem since the Khor Dubai "announcement" six weeks ago – apart from branding our Deira cultural complex *Theatre Land*. He himself is working on preparations for new large-scale enterprises in China and Vietnam. Al Adheem has prioritized its projects. First in line are those announced by the ruler and of central economic significance, for which the funding has already been secured. Then there are those for which we do not yet have financing, but which have the ruler's blessing. Finally, there are the proposals that remain undecided. The Deira complex ranks somewhere off the bottom of the list. It has zero priority.

Culture is just one issue among many, after all, and this city is a family business with its decisions taken by the head – a contract for the Creek extension today, another few man-made islands tomorrow. Transposed to the Europe of medieval feudalism, The Boss's office is the manorial great hall with Emiratis and expert special advisers the loyal retinue, maintaining prestige, scurrying about for opportunities and enterprises to satisfy the master's ambition: for Dubai to be Number One, to stand out as a unique 21st-century paragon of urban development. Project teams fly their colours on the threshold of the 52nd floor and joust for land rights for their developments. Having already received preliminary permits for specified lots and passed several levels up the decision-making process, they are now jostling for that elusive and infinitely precious opportunity: the chance to seize a minute with the ruler or at least with The Boss; the chance of a nudge for that stalled project that is a new airport here, a hotel chain there. Fifty-two floors of the building busily engaged in producing and evaluating ideas, an enormous magic flute of a place needing just the right managerial puff through it to make the enchanting melody of the city's economic and social development issue forth.

Pity the ruler! The poor man is hounded constantly by his own people, each craving his signature and blessing for the next great technological feat in the race for complete mobilization of this city's

enormous potentialities. Is there anyone else who governs a city where so much has yet to be decided? In a place where everything depends not only on a single authority but on a single individual, there can only be one solution: total deregulation, of course! If such a person is to be able to turn his back on any of his own businesses for a second, that is. Confidence in confidants is good, competition is better. Open everything up to market forces! Divide and conquer!

I tell Azad that we have to jog the ruler's memory about the Deira complex. He lets out a laugh. If anyone is in a position to remind him, he says, it's me.

15 May

Bouman is relaxed on the telephone. Unlike the Australian at the project management company. He calls every Wednesday, makes his enquiries and drums it in that with every week that passes we incur another two-week delay. The market is going from frantic to frenzied. The idea of a Pavilion ready to open in the next year is now unthinkable. Where are we supposed to exhibit and perform, then? With the exception of the new funding guarantee for *Muslim Faces*, there is no further word about funds to work with.

Meanwhile, Frau Sturzenegger, an exuberant chemical blonde in her fifties from St Gallen in Switzerland, has materialized here with an exhibition designer. Frau Sturzenegger has an extremely un-Swiss way of telling it like it is. Greeting me on the 28th floor she quips: "So this is the team of amateurs you're tackling culture with." Our "location scout" Khalil runs through the pros and cons of various exhibition venues available. The unused foyer at the entrance to an underground boulevard in the International Finance Centre seems the most promising. You enter the foyer through revolving doors and down the escalators. Radiating from this space are avenues on different levels housing Mexican, Chinese and Italian fast food joints, the office of a school of economics, and a smattering of travel agencies and car rental offices. We stand in the foyer as every nationality under the sun streams past to the next appointment armed with briefcases and bags, laptops, iPods and paper cups of coffee on the go. Frau Sturzenegger contemplates the scene and whispers to the designer. It is evident already that working with the boulevard's "Facility Management" department won't be easy. Finding a janitor or technician able to give us a bit of information about security, electrical connections and so on is proving difficult. Even Salem's intervention at senior management level comes to nothing. "Well, Uzbekistan was no picnic either," remarks Frau Sturzenegger.

But the tenor of her visit is positive. A contract proposal goes to management; the budget appears to be approved. A big European publisher is interested in the catalogue. Mona and Latifa have enlarged a few of the photographs and affixed them to the glass wall of my goldfish bowl of an office. There's one of an old *badawi* by a mosque in Medina; a Yemeni bride in full regalia, perched on a high stool and staring po-faced at the camera; and a shot of men saddling up and loading a caravan of camels.

16 May

I hear voices approaching. Suddenly, they're standing in my goldfish bowl – Salem and a six-footer in wide braces with an even wider grin. Winston. On decibel count alone, I'd say he has the larynx of a Bryn Terfel. Salem, however, introduces him as the city's other culture expert. Winston cocks his head to one side, with breathtaking condescension plants his tennis-racquet-sized hand on my shoulder, and adds: "But not in your ballpark". Winston, according to Salem, works for the International Finance Centre and other clients in the holding company. I feign interest. Our culture expert relinquishes all restraint. He's from Waco (Texas) but has been here for some time. He has lived in Manila and Singapore, Zimbabwe, Buenos Aires, Moscow and Frankfurt; his wife is Spanish and living in Vancouver though she's enthusiastic about the idea of moving here. Winston, this Superman of consultants, has flown to the aid of helpless governments everywhere and hauled them from the brink of the cultureless void. Thanks to Winston, and his employer McKinsey, impoverished cities and countries the world over are now considerably better off. Oh, really? Zimbabwe? Manila? Have I missed something? I ask him what he did in Frankfurt. Oh, that was another thing altogether; Frankfurt already had culture. You don't say. In Frankfurt he was responsible for setting up the office of the European Central Bank.

Winston loves people in all their diversity; he loves the world, which is why he came to this city. "How is it possible *not* to love this city?" he trumpets. "That's how I see it! Such an awesome melting pot of nationalities and languages!" Winston speaks them all, as you might expect, and he demonstrates his linguistic prowess with a "Gehzoonhaight" when I sneeze, meaning "Gesundheit" of course. And what is it that Winston is actually doing for this city in the International Finance Centre, apart from loving the world and all the nations thereof? Ah, setting up an art investment fund. That figures. Christie's has already expressed interest, a few local banks are definitely in and the rest Winston will win over with a tailor-made presentation for the private members of the Capital Club. It's just dazzling here when it comes to rustling up private initiative! For lack of time I can do no more than passively agree. It was nice meeting you, bellows Winston, finally releasing my shoulder. He lays his massive palm on the hapless Salem and together they vacate my autonomous zone – which, only now does it dawn on me, is under serious threat.

It comes to mind that I've heard of Winston before. Latifa tells me that senior management confuses the two of us on occasion, whenever they are engaged in a project that requires the input of cultural experts. Now I really am curious, grab the business card he left on my desk and google him. I can't find anything about him, apart from a student photo with a blonde, full-bosomed Jane (who is almost certainly not from Spain). But then I check the International Finance Centre homepage and there he is, listed as Special Projects Adviser. His curriculum vitae reads pretty much as he related it to me (Manila, Zimbabwe etc) though I see he failed to mention the most interesting detail: Winston went to drama school and is a consulting board member, naturally, of the Waco Community Theatre. An expert indeed.

18 May

Receive a surprise email from Pink. He's in town tomorrow, as I probably know, to discuss the Met satellite broadcasts. With whom, I wonder? I know nothing about it.

19 May

Make arrangements to meet Pink for dinner at a Lebanese restaurant on the top floor of the Emirates Towers Hotel, after a ping-pong game of missed calls and voice messages on our mobile phones. He's already been given the standard VIP tour of the city: the helicopter flight, the Rolls Royce limousine service and a few minutes with The Boss, evidently in the company of Salem, who has made no mention of it. I arrive on the 57th floor around eight and, as the Russian hostess shows me to our table, I can hear across the restaurant that Pink is not alone. Winston! Pink waves over at me and takes a few steps towards me as Winston hauls himself up to his full height and yells my name, excitedly, as though some cleaver-wielding assassin is about to ambush me from behind. I swerve sharply to greet Pink, thereby avoiding the crushing weight of Winston's hand landing on my shoulder. Fat chance of unwinding over a quiet drink with Pink, then. For some inexplicable, possibly patriotic, reason Winston finds it appropriate to introduce me to Pink as if I were meeting him by sheer coincidence and for the first time. He follows with a little speech on the significance of the Met to occidental culture in general and to Manhattan in particular. I wonder if the two have bumped into each other by chance and if this buffoon of a consultant is settling in to amuse us for the entire evening. Pink takes it easy, leans back in his chair and allows his gaze to sweep back and forth between Winston and me. So I too lean back and wait to see what's coming. It turns out to be Winston's self-promoting speech of introduction – how he's worked all over the world, how enamoured he is of people of all cultures. Ah, so they have only just met. I resolve to introduce my new friend Winston to other people in exactly the way he does it himself (Manila, Singapore, etc etc …). I wonder if he'd notice.

I can't help but ask if the two are known to each other or whether they've just met by chance, and see from the corner of my eye that Winston reacts with a hesitant shake of the head as Pink responds immediately – their paths crossed briefly this morning on the 52nd floor and Winston offered to show him the mall with the ski slope. Yes, I can imagine my colleague might be quite the tour guide. He has already given a guided tour of the mall to the General Secretary of UNESCO, he tells us, and to Tiger Woods, who had just five minutes to spare to buy a suit at Harvey Nichols for a reception in his honour at the American Embassy in Abu Dhabi.

Pink has spotted that Winston and I are not exactly bosom pals and wonders aloud if I knew that he was an actor. Whatever the reason, Winston is disinclined to elaborate. Instead we talk about how *fantastic* the city is, or rather Winston does. I'm starting to get fidgety and ask him if he'd like to join us for a meal. But of course I have underestimated him. It has dawned on him at last that I don't like him. His grin remains fixed, but there is no mistaking the frost in his eyes as he leans in close to confide, in a hushed tone, the reason why he won't be even sticking his nose in the menu: he has a videoconference this evening with his friends from the Waco theatre. I feel mildly guilty. We stand to shake hands. Winston promises Pink that he will definitely visit on his next trip to the Big Apple, though Pink has extended no such invitation.

Alone at last, we make no further mention of the city's other cultural expert. Of greater interest to me is the reason for Pink's visit and I learn about his invitation to a concert by a popular Chinese pianist at the ruler's palace. A member of the Met's Advisory Board is also the ruler's lawyer, apparently, and this gentleman considers it important to foster close cultural ties between New York and Dubai and to encourage Emiratis to appreciate and learn about classical music and opera. Pink is relatively new to opera management and has put the wind up some of his regular donors with his fresh ideas about contemporary staging, as well as unsettling his European colleagues with the Met's bold plans to exploit new media to broaden the appeal and commercial viability of opera. His dry anecdotes of bizarre exchanges with the more conservative flank of opera devotees and the equally intransigent proponents of cutting-edge modernism give me to think he quite probably enjoys the role of cultural agitator, swinging like a pendulum between business and the avant-garde. Our city suits him just fine, cementing his reputation in this respect while opening a new business stream for his opera house at home. And he's entertaining with it, pursing his lips in imitation of his insulted colleagues and pushing the bridge of his unnervingly large spectacles up his nose with a twinkle in his eye as he speaks of some singer.

Pink seems to have been impressed by both the ruling family and by his brief conversation with The Boss. And then he discloses that Matthieu visited him at the Met ten days ago and cajoled him into this visit where he promptly negotiated a contract for live cinema broadcasts of opera premiers. As to whether he knew I had already broached this topic with Pink in connection with our introductory programme for the Deira complex, Pink tells me Matthieu said that it had been arranged that he would be taking over the project. For a moment I consider letting Pink in on all the dirt, not least to give him an idea of what might be in store for him. But he seems thrilled at how things are working out for him. So rather than rain on his parade I do no more than hint that collaboration is sometimes difficult here because communications don't always work and you never know who is listening and getting in on the act behind the scenes. More lip-pursing from Pink. And suddenly we don't have much left to say to each other – probably because we both know that I no longer have much say in the matter. We promise to keep each other in the loop.

20 May

I call Salem, even though it's the weekend, unable to contain my anger about the Met thing any longer. He says he didn't know much about it. He had been called up to the 52nd floor to meet an important cultural manager and was told Matthieu had already met this man previously to speak about the cinema screenings. He hadn't remembered until afterwards that I had already suggested this project and that Pink was the very same opera director I had spoken about.

Salem is no novice when it comes to avoiding direct questions, as I'm learning from experience. And he's nervous. I can see I'm going to have to put a gun to his head. I tell him to see to it that Matthieu keeps his hands off the Met. But as our agitated discussion crescendoes and fades, I realize that I have infinitely overestimated Salem's influence on the matter. They involve him when they have to and tell him only what he needs to know. We both know it. We both know how little, if anything, he can or is allowed to reveal about what is really going on on the 52nd floor. So Matthieu wins by a knockout. That rankles. Roll on the Director-General.

21 May

A breathless call from Salem around lunchtime. I am to make my way over to the Rashid Hall in the World Trade Centre as quickly as possible; the ruler will be there in a few minutes expecting to sign off on the Khor Dubai concept. Breathlessness is the only response to news like this.

The Trade Centre building has a shopping mall of a foyer with exhibition halls to left and right. The Rashid Hall is barricaded with a huge white advertising hoarding with the Al Adheem logo scrawled across it and a montage of the historic photos of pearl divers and so forth we saw at the announcement ceremony seven weeks ago. A crowd of Emiratis and as many foreigners are gathered in front of it, about a hundred people in all, most of them Al Adheem employees. The mainly younger men in *dishdash*es are sitting on sofas, their ceremonial camel sticks between their knees, chatting animatedly among themselves, eyeing every suit that approaches with suspicion. Salem is nowhere to be seen, nor are any other local notables. The foreigners stand around at bar tables where refreshments are served. Every once in a while a wide door in the hoarding swings open and one of the Al Adheem marketing staff emerges from the hall, blinking and enveloped in a cloud of incense, suggesting the fire of another little event has been lit. We await the ruler's arrival.

At this point Marwan swaggers into the foyer, his massive form cutting a swathe through the crowd. He's accompanied by a gaggle of minions and is, as usual, jabbering into the mobile phone planted conspicuously on his left cheek. He shakes hands with the young Emiratis who have bounced to their feet, rushes past the foreign personnel and disappears behind a wall. He reappears some fifteen minutes later, with a retinue that now includes Salem, who directs a discreet shrug my way. An acknowledgement like this, under such circumstances, is something new, and I recognize it as a breach of unwritten protocol.

The Marwan brigade, Salem included, moves towards the far entrance. The press-ganged audience hangs on, standing around until fit to drop, shooting the breeze about nothing. I know virtually no one here and cast an envious glance at the young men in *dishdash*es making a stealthy retreat to the car park. It has been at least an hour, after all, since they first flopped down onto the sofas. There's another half-hour of orange juice, figs and the smallest of small talk before word gets round that the ruler will not be coming and the whole thing is cancelled.

But then, all of a sudden, it's on again. Salem calls late that afternoon and persuades me to give it another go. And why not? I expect there'll be many more needlessly wasted hours ahead of me. From a distance, I catch sight of The Boss standing by the entrance to the Trade Centre, looming over the crowd, Marwan close at hand. Salem is on the step below them. They're doubtless waiting for the arrival of His Highness, completely untroubled by the 40°C heat outside, resisting any temptation to take three steps backwards into the comfort of the conditioned air behind the sliding glass doors. What's a little sweating, now and then, in the service of the ruler?

I give the group a half-hearted wave and make my way to the foyer. There are even more people than before gathered in front of the Al Adheem hoarding, Emiratis for the most part. The word is that His Highness flew to Kuwait this morning for the funeral of a member of the ruling family and is now expected any minute. There's a good chance he really will come this time, given The Boss is here. It is 8.30 in the evening by the time the ruler, in his dark-blue robe, the Crown Prince, The Boss and the rest of the entourage head for the brightly lit and lately deserted lobby. Meanwhile, the invited audience has arranged itself into two lines by the door, the *dishdash* crew jostling for position. Winston's there, of course, standing right up front, craning his pink chin in the Sheikh's direction and giving him a firm nod though, surrounded by the usual TV crews, the ruler pays attention only to his compatriots, greeting them with tired eyes and a quiet *As-salaamu 'alaykum*. Then everyone heads through the door and into the dimmed Rashid Hall, with its irritating lounge music tootling away while the intended live musicians fumble ineffectually with cables and microphones in the background. The

architect's model has been assembled on the floor this time and it's possible to walk round it.

Not much has changed since the last presentation; there are the same toy replicas of massed wind-tower houses ranged along the Creek, interspersed with tufts of plastic vegetation and palm trees. The ruler appears displeased about something. I can neither see him in the crowd nor hear him amid the hubbub, but judging by the way Marwan scuttles in, fiddling with his *ghutra*, his head hanging submissively, the ruler is running short on enthusiasm. As if to confirm my impression, those leading the group suddenly turn hard about, sowing confusion among the entourage, and His Highness cleaves his way stony-faced through the aghast, recoiling multitude, with The Boss, Marwan and the other dignitaries and acolytes trailing forlornly in his wake. Out of curiosity, I text Salem to find out what happened, but answer comes there none. Which, oddly, puts me at ease. Perhaps someone has put a stop to all this real estate nonsense tied up with the Khor Dubai project. But, if so, what is there actually left?

25 May

Mustafa invites me to a desert party. We don't know each other especially well. He's a freelance headhunter who specializes in finding CEOs and he has just offered his services to recruit departmental managers for the new Cultural Council. We met at one of the countless schmoozing events on Dubai's eternal cocktail party circuit and have had lunch a few times since. I understand Mustafa is the son of one of the richest bankers in the country and is the sole occupant (barring his staff) of a fifteen-room villa near the Mall of the Emirates, with a zoo in the garden housing several wildcats and a collection of large reptiles. He's a nice boy of around forty with pale eyes and a rosy complexion who is slight of stature and thinning on top. He may not be everyone's idea of a desert Adonis but there's always an ultra-chic girl in her early twenties by his side. If he is as successful a hunter of CEOs as he is of exotic, good-looking women then I reckon we should sign him up on an exclusive contract straight away.

Since I'm not responsible for personnel or contractual matters, I have no qualms about accepting his invitation. I park my Polo at a lonely petrol station and a four-by-four chauffeur service takes me to the camp. At the end of the twenty-minute drive we come to a bowl-shaped hollow in the sands, a circlet of dunes up to thirty metres high surrounding a space that vibrates to the pounding beat of Arab pop music. The camp is set up on the lines of a traditional encampment, with a carpet runner flanked by stands of fruit and vegetables at the end of which an attendant greets guests. Custom would suggest that role should fall to the host but Mustafa, it seems, is no slave to convention.

Someone hands me a refresher towel and, by the time I have wiped the grains of sand from the corners of my eyes, Mustafa's younger sister Layla has materialized before me. With her metal-rimmed glasses, long strawberry blonde hair and full-cheeked face she looks a little like Janis Joplin. We have never met before but by her third sentence I have discovered that she adores her brother for his gaiety and unconventional approach and is well used to providing follow-up care to his discarded girlfriends. With a dismissive wave of her hand as if to say the girlfriend thing is old hat, she goes on to fill me in on who has been invited and where I can find something to eat and drink. This she has to scream in my ear, as the DJ is really pumping now. The atmosphere is pretty wild already, though the sun has only just disappeared behind the dunes and the guests can't have been here long. Layla, like Janis Joplin, has a good pair of lungs and I learn that Mustafa spends a good part of the year in London, New York, the Maldives and in the Swiss mountains (CEO spotting, doubtless) – places that are home to his guests, or regularly frequented by them at least, for much the same reasons as himself I suspect. We mingle. I of course know no one, see hardly a *dishdash* or *abaya*, but gather from Layla that almost half of those present are Emirati.

She introduces me to Fatma, Sergei, Paolo and Niloufar, who are dressed in up-to-the-minute street fashion costing thousands of dollars, the girls subtly tanned with choppy-cut hair, their tender cheeks preserved with the latest La Prairie Black Caviar products. The young men have probably come straight from the Korean masseur and the single ones sport the tousled locks of the just-woken bedroom look; those with wives or girlfriends have gone for the slicked-back macho style of John Travolta in *Pulp Fiction*. They kiss and hug one another in fulsome greeting and buzz their way over reed matting and through an obstacle course of bar counters and barbecue grills to a horse-shoe seating area strewn with carpets and cushions at the foot of the rising dunes. At the centre of it all is a dance floor, with Mustafa briefing the DJ at a Technics turntable. He waves at me excitedly, but he is too busy to chat.

Two-thirds of all the women present are on the dance floor and I can see now that a few of them are European. A light Riesling is doing the rounds and I settle back on the cushions with Layla where we toast her brother and the whole raucous assembly, as the lamplight projects the writhing dancers' silhouettes onto the dunes like a shadow theatre show.

Once the dancing really gets going, Mustafa takes over the

microphone and announces a competition for the women. The one to get to the top of the highest dune first wins a Gucci handbag. No one's killed in the rush because for Arab women, especially those who live in the Gulf, walking is something undertaken only in the air-conditioned necessity of getting from shop to shop. Nonetheless, about fifteen brave souls head towards the starting line. Mustafa has a bit of fun with them, calling the women back twice for alleged false starts, then they're off again gamely slithering their way up the dune to the sound of heavy house music as the audience cheers them on. Three Arab ladies (Egyptians, Layla says, with a slightly mocking grin) rapidly fall behind and wade back down giggling hysterically. Maneli, a woman of Iranian mountain stock, takes the lead though her winning form can't necessarily be ascribed to her origins: as she's awarded the prize she gasps into the microphone that she's lived in Dubai since she was a child.

Cue more dancing until Mustafa announces the next round of games. This time he entreats the ladies to take to the floor in a contest for the most elegant, erotic dancer, to be judged by the assembled males. There's more interest this time, in direct pro-portion to the value of the prize: a 16-carat gold Cavalli Triptic dress watch. Such is the spontaneous surge of bodies and the throng circling the dance floor that I have to get up from my cushions to catch something of the show. The weaker competitors are clapped off stage after one or two songs, but an English woman makes it as far as the final round with a pretty professional striptease, running out of steam only when she's down to a bikini made of imitation roses. Mustafa pulls her over to the microphone for a chat: she's from Birmingham and on vacation (although from what, she doesn't say) and seems to know Mustafa pretty well already. But it's Reem, Mustafa's youngest sister, who wins the Cavalli. Thinner than Layla and taller than Mustafa, she performs a fabulous belly dance, her home-game advantage giving her a bit of an edge in trouncing the competition. The handbag was handed over without much ceremony, but the watch is presented in a package fashioned like a shiny beetle, and large enough to contain a Christmas turkey.

Later on Mustafa calls on the men to test their skills, with Elvira the professional belly dancer. She is well known and admired in this milieu judging by the sustained applause that greets her even before she takes the floor. The winner in Elvira's judgement will receive a MacBook White. She dances with three partners at a time, one after the other, and indicates which one goes through to the next round by encircling the happy man in a flawless solo performance. A chorus rises from the audience with each solo, reaching a climax of whooping and yowling in appreciation of Elvira's talents.

She moves as if in a trance, with half-closed eyes, and no one doubts her verdicts are based purely on professional criteria. The party reaches its height. Dancers flounder in ever more bizarre contortions, egged on by the onlookers embracing one another as though in celebration of a cup final win; the dunes resound with yells and the maudlin vocals of an Egyptian pop diva and even the Filipino serving staff are compelled to push in closer to catch a glimpse of the fun. After several sweaty rounds during which each man proves himself surprisingly nifty at whirling on his own axis as well as

around the belly dancer, the Mac goes to the brawny Samir, a schoolmate of Mustafa's from London who's getting a little heavy around the haunches.

By midnight the mood has subsided to mellow, everyone satiated with food and drink and exhausted from the dancing. A few couples arrange rides back to the city; others disappear behind the dunes. All of a sudden, the belly dancer plonks herself down between Layla and me and I chat with her as she puffs away on a *sheesha*. She doesn't talk much but seems to be a good pal of Layla's. She's from Venice, she says, and studied ballet as a child. She had her first experience of belly dancing in Cairo at fifteen. Eleven years of active service was enough, apparently. From the way she tells it, a belly-dancing career induces as much stress as working in the accident and emergency department of a general hospital.

It's no surprise to learn that Mustafa has been a loyal customer for years, one whom Elvira cannot refuse even though she's now in retirement. I look up to see him still on stage with the DJ, hopping about with a blonde girl, looking completely spent but happy. The crescent moon sinks over the kebab grill and disappears behind the dunes.

28 May

An air of unease in the team. No one has received their monthly salary cheque – no one in the entire government, reportedly. Bad news for the young people living hand-to-mouth on luxurious necessities. Now they'll be forced to appeal to their mothers to make ends meet. Latifa claims to have found out that the earliest anyone will be paid is a month from now, because supposedly changes to the payroll system cannot be made at short notice ... the personnel department, run entirely by Emiratis, appears to be particularly adept at inducing meltdowns. I've heard of files disappearing, employees receiving the wrong copies of their contracts, and various other muddles contributing to the general chaos. Even now they're holding a "Promising Leaders" workshop in the conference rooms on our floor. The current head of department is unlikely to be one of them. He and I became acquainted during my contract negotiations – a gentle individual who doesn't speak particularly good English and who regarded me from under his *ghutra* with a gaze so sorrowful that it is engraved indelibly on my memory. Perhaps he'd already seen it coming. He's being eased out, a complex procedure in this country. Most probably he won't be fired but redeployed in another post. Presumably he's also failed to pay himself.

6

1 June

Asked around in the personnel department to find out who the new personnel boss is, and got three different answers. No shortage of Promising Leaders, then. Salary will be paid on the 25th of the month at the earliest. All being well.

Latifa doesn't seem to get on with the people in charge of technical facilities and building management at the International Finance Centre. And Khalil says he has already spoken to four different people in an effort to get the floorplan of the foyer, with no success so far. But I only discover these things after Frau Sturzenegger calls me, having received no response to her emails to my Emirati colleagues. She reproaches herself for not having taken care of these things personally. I expect she's learnt from how she had to do things in Uzbekistan. I promise to see to it myself.

Looks like our consul-general, duly alerted, had promised to do the same – some time ago. His previous inquiries must have drawn a blank too. Now he strides into the International Finance Centre armed with a folding ruler. He calls me during a meeting and asks careful questions about the parts of the foyer we're using for the exhibition. We compare notes about the foyer space, the number of steps from the down escalator to the revolving door, lifts for wheelchair access, and so on. I have a go at describing all the wall surfaces we need to take into consideration; he paces them out, cellphone to his ear, ruler in hand. The man takes all of this in his stride, explaining that he regards it as his job to bring his personal commitment to cultural projects. He says this in all sincerity, with no trace of irony.

2 June

Sheikh Mansour has a new plan. Salem asks me to give him a call. The decision about his design centre will not be made before the second half of the year, he explains on the phone. How does he know this? And what, exactly, is the significance of the timing? He waits for my reaction. I wait for him to go on. Mansour tells me he has spoken to his architect, Zold, and they have designed a project that will fit in very well with the Khor Dubai development. Another pause. I continue to listen. He outlines the plan: an amphitheatre and art centre all under one domed glass roof with a barge alongside which can be used as a stage or to house an exhibition cube. I'm astounded by the piracy; roof apart, the idea has been lifted wholesale from the design I developed with Bouman. I ask His Highness if he recalls the presentation we made on 1 May in his presence, in particular the section about the preliminary performance area developed for us by the Belgian architect Bouman, which offered similar (I err on the side of diplomacy) facilities to the design he now proposes. But he's having none of it. "I have a compleeetely different location in mind; the design has nooothing to do with Bouman," he says, exaggerating his vowels to the point of self-parody. The project is in line with his business model for the design centre, he insists, and is to serve as a launch site for design and cinema. A "launch site"? Well, wasn't that the whole point of our Pavilion? His Highness sounds almost petulant now. Why won't I get in touch with his architect? Zold is more than willing to come to town anytime and present his ideas. The Boss, he cannot resist adding, would also welcome it.

6 June

Museum directors from Germany, who refer to themselves bizarrely as "the three generals" (two of them are nearing retirement), are visiting under the auspices of the German Ministry of Foreign Affairs and are accompanied by the amiable consul-general. I'm not sure what impression they're making on the Emiratis since it's all a bit more official than has been the case with visitors from the United States, Great Britain, Singapore and Italy. Culture types tend to come to the Emirates Towers in camouflage and generally dress and behave like business people. The Germans by contrast are somewhat idio-syncratic. Professors address one another by their formal titles and there's a whiff of academia, not to mention eccentricity, hanging about the group. Their speech is ponderous and considered, and there's not the slightest danger that one of them will fish a USB from his briefcase and project a PowerPoint presentation on the wall. Instead, they pass around lavishly illustrated catalogues of their museums and collections. Old-fashioned it may be, but refreshingly so.

Things seem to be going well. We introduce our (preliminary) strategy and go into a little more detail about the museum planning. The generals are interested but cautious and, I sense, new to this arena. They want to sound us out. I know they are travelling on to Qatar and Abu Dhabi and they will almost certainly want to sound them out there too. I'm afraid (or I'm hoping) they might be a little too late and that other national institutions have already staked their claims in those places.

7 June

The Abu Dhabi people do things better. They have more money and possibly a better idea of what to do with it, in terms of culture. A renowned (East) German orchestra is to perform pieces by Wagner, several for the first time. As soon as I enter the auditorium, I feel as though I'm in the Deutsche Oper in Berlin. At least two-thirds of the audience are sixty or over and look like regular aficionados. And all of them speak German! Nearby is a little coterie of English,

French, Russians and Italians. A middle-aged French woman leans over a gentleman in a *dishdash* in the row in front of her and asks him why he is here. The man replies that he is interested in classical music. She springs back in her seat and calls approvingly to a friend sitting three rows behind, "He's interested in classical music!" as she stabs downwards with her index finger at her neighbour.

Eleven Emirati bigwigs are sitting in the front row. A few women in *abaya*s are sitting in mine – giggling and swapping text messages on their cellphones and then disappearing during the intermission. The programme notes have been written by a German professor who has included an essay on Wagner in the context of the early Romantic period. This is apparently of interest to people here. The event is being covered onstage and from various points in the auditorium by two German national television crews, ensuring no one at home misses this musical triumph, this desert invasion by the stormtroopers of German high culture. Enlightenment through Wagner's *Zukunftsmusik*, his *Music of the Future*.

10 June

Another visit from Germany. This time it's a delegation from the Bavarian state government. The consul-general gets in touch a few days beforehand to ask for help, because no one from the government here seems prepared to receive the Bavarian prime minister. I go over Salem's head and get through to The Boss's office where Bavaria means nothing to anyone. Mention of BMW solves the problem and The Boss extends a warm welcome to our distinguished visitor from Munich, who has his education minister and one of the three museum "generals" in tow. We even manage to fit in a brief discussion between The Boss and the education minister. The minister points to his "general" and says the man gives him much food for thought because he is always coming up with creative ideas. And creative ideas cost money. The man seems a bit thrown by the minister's irony. Afterwards, The Boss takes me to one side and asks with concern whether the museum plan isn't just a black hole that will consume vast amounts of cash. It's the first time I've had a few minutes with him to speak about the commercial viability of a World Museum. I have such figures at my fingertips and give him an estimate of the building and operating costs, and the production processes involved if we are to make something serious of it. I also reel off a few comparable figures I have in my head from the preparation I'd done for earlier presentations: figures for the Louvre, the British Museum, the Metropolitan, and museums in Berlin and Abu Dhabi. As I'm stepping into the lift with the Bavarians, The Boss purses his lips and squeezes my hand tightly. I detect a particularly pointed look, as if he's alerting me to the fact that we have a problem.

12 June

Discussions with the museums and the German Ministry of Foreign Affairs continue. They are prepared to collaborate – no concerns about criticism from the more conservative cultural camp at home. I propose to Salem that we extend an official invitation and seal the deal on the project. The ceremony is to take place in three weeks, just before the summer holidays start. First we'll all have a meeting with The Boss to endorse the guidelines regarding the requirements for partnership (including consultation on construction, exhibitions, training for Emirati employees, building the collection, research). Then both parties will sign a strategic partnership agreement in front of the cameras.

I'm still waiting for fallout from the 52nd floor but it fails to appear. Seems people are warming to the idea of a World Museum with German and, subsequently, international involvement.

13 June

At a morning meeting on the future of the libraries I meet the institutions' director, Hamid Al Shemti. In passing, I mention the International Literary Festival which opens that afternoon at the

Intercontinental on the Creek. The festival is the brainchild of an English woman (who set up a bookshop after marrying an Emirati and moving here in the late '60s) and a friend of hers who is director of Foyles bookshop. Sponsored by the national airline, the festival is being held under the patronage of the ruler's son. Seventy authors, many of them well-known, are expected from fifteen Western and Arab countries, and there is an impressive range of fringe events. Hamid gives me a slightly bewildered look. This is the first he's heard of it. The meeting with us was convened because the libraries want something from us: money and structural support. Few books are purchased; the inventory is piteous, to say nothing of the lending figures. Most of the facilities are in poor condition. Libraries represent the dog-eared corners of an otherwise flawlessly glossy picture of this 21st-century consumer society. With our help, this could change. Apart from a few friendly words, nothing much comes of the meeting.

15 June

I am unable to hold out against yet another office move. Down, this time, to the 21st floor. A sign of demotion? The new office is even bigger, though our team hasn't grown since our move up to the 28th floor. Each of us has twice as much space as before. Salem can offer no explanation for the move other than the suggestion of a potential increase in staff numbers. The only increase I've seen up until now has been in the number of emails flooding in and in the pending pile on my desk. They'll have to put in partition walls so that I can work with fewer distractions, if such a thing is possible.

16 June

The partition walls are installed but now my office sprawls over 150 square metres, about half the room. The Indian foreman shakes his head (in other words he agrees with me) when I tell him he has to take it all down again.

17 June

The thermometer climbs above forty-five degrees. A hot and humid wind blows through the byways of Sheikh Zayed Road, giving rise to a noxious pea-souper that coats your eyeballs and mucous membranes as soon as you step out of the car. Asian cleaning ladies waiting at the bus stop, or making their exhausted way on foot to the next job, take shelter under black umbrellas, a flimsy defence against the torrid heat of the haze-cloaked sun. Just two minutes under this doom-laden sky, which radiates not sunshine but a kind of miasma, is enough to soak your shirt so it clings to you as if after a swim. So irradiated are the roof-top water tanks that hotter water issues from the cold tap than from the hot, and beach showers have been decommissioned as a precaution against scalding. The sea has warmed up to body temperature. Any hope of a bracing swim is dashed by immersion in a warm, soporific brine that induces nothing friskier than enervation and languor.

Vacation time looms. Soon, the residents of Dubai will flock in their hundreds of thousands to the cooler climes of the Mediterranean, Europe and California. The luxury hotels here will flood the market with bargain rates enticing tens of thousands of tourists, who find the idea of living in a forty-square-metre room with continental breakfast and a view of the chilled pool for a hundred euros a night such astonishingly good value that they are unfazed by their five-star virtual imprisonment.

19 June

The Boss has been appointed head of the central banking authority, I read in the *Gulf News*. His expression in the photo is impassive. This is now his sixth mandate. Apparently those who enjoy the ruler's trust are a select few. I can understand that. But burdening the trusted with so many responsibilities that they can no longer see where they're going seems to me not the best way to go about things. Or is it that the trusted few are piling it on themselves, grabbing every opportunity to increase their power and influence?

Still no news on a Director-General for the Cultural Council. We're making almost no progress because every step (hiring personnel, contract negotiation, transferring money, approving travel) is executed at the speed of Sheikh Zayed chugging over the dunes in his Jeep forty years ago. Salem is definitely not being considered for the post. What role will he be playing in the future, then? I admit I can't imagine the work without him and he's the only person in this game I trust. Is that because he has no power? Or because he is too fine a person for crooked dealings? Or is he? (bearing in mind the opera broadcasting business). I am sure he had counted on being appointed. Talking once to Latifa, he proclaimed himself a soldier loyal and true of the ruler, ready for any task His Highness might have in store. But what if His Highness doesn't have anything in store, but instead leaves him with us and allows him to languish here without guidance?

Around noon I spot The Boss in the boulevard near the escalator. He waves a greeting, then changes his mind and approaches me. He accepts my congratulations with chin held high, but it's the World Museum he wants to talk about. I tell him the museum people have been invited to attend next Sunday and someone's working on the contract for the signing, for which he will need to be present. He knows this, of course, but he now has a little surprise for me: the museum has to make money. This is the first I've heard of it. He explains how he wants to achieve that, or rather how he wants us to achieve it. The Western partner museums get the land for free; we raise the finance for building and for the museum's operating and exhibition costs. I own up to my doubts about this and suggest we discuss it properly as soon as possible. I don't think our current position amongst the strolling shoppers and assorted business people is the right venue for serious discussion of a project of this magnitude. But The Boss doesn't have the time. He considers the matter settled by virtue of letting me know. The rest – making the museum profitable with partners who take in hundreds of millions in state subsidies every year – is now up to me. I make a final attempt to voice my concern that his plan runs contrary to the nature of

public museums, which are generally state-subsidized. Why would the taxpayer or donor in Germany, Russia or Great Britain agree to his money being spent in our city? This objection has The Boss reeling to face me again. "We in Dubai," he says, with his face unexpectedly close to mine, "don't play by the old rules. This city rewrites the rules! What's true for commerce will be true for culture. It's time the Cultural Council stopped talking about how things were done in the past and started showing how culture can be built in the future, without financial support." I tell him I cannot share his opinion. The Boss fixes me with another of his pointed looks: "Think about it," he says. "The decision is not up to me alone. But it is my opinion."

22 June
"His Highness Sheikh Mohammed bin Rashid Al Maktoum, Vice President and Prime Minister of the United Arab Emirates and ruler of Dubai, has made known his will to build a World Museum. Unique collections from renowned museums across the world will be brought together in one place for the first time in the history of mankind. In doing so, the Museum will bear witness to the ruler's vision of building a global centre that will draw the world's most significant artists and artworks to the city."

According to the press release to be issued today. Less grandiloquence would have been better, but Salem urged me not to interfere. In any event, I only caught sight of the draft by chance as late as yesterday evening.

The announcement means that the signing of the contract is a foregone conclusion, though the ruler will not be attending the signing ceremony in person. The consul-general and I meet the museum directors at their hotel opposite the Emirates Tower. The gentlemen arrived late last night and are still seated in the restaurant, leaning back from the remains of their breakfast, when we arrive. We end up talking about the lack of a unifying theme, given that the museums are from different cities and have a variety of names.

What's missing is a common identity. German federalism totters for a moment as the generals seriously consider the idea of referring to themselves as the United German Museums when appearing together abroad. A lively and unprofessorial exchange ensues until someone remembers that this is a decision that would need to be cleared by their respective ministers of education. In other words, it will be a while before the branding can begin. For now it's going to have to stay the way it is: the museums of Berlin, Dresden, Munich, in neutral alphabetical order.

We drive over to the Tower and take the lift to the 52nd floor. The Boss shows up a mere ten minutes after the appointed time and booms his deafening greetings as usual. He stresses how aware he is that one must learn from historic institutions such as those present how new cultural facilities can be built and funded. Someone must have encouraged him to reconsider his plan to rewrite the rules of this particular game. A few minutes later, though, he makes a remark that unnerves me once more: "We must all of us make an effort to ensure the World Museum is a *win-win* proposition." Yes, they love that here. Win-win situations. One triumph is not enough; both sides take the laurels. Except Dubai's partner wins only in the sense that failure is not an option, success is the only possible outcome. Perhaps he has rewritten the rules after all.

That evening we dine in the same Lebanese restaurant where Pink and I last met, high above the city's rooftop antennae. Sure enough, Winston waves from one of the neighbouring tables and loudly calls my name. Luckily, he shows no sign of coming over. The museum people seem sleepy but satisfied with the day's events. There's no further need for serious discussion at this point. Plans will be developed over the next few weeks with a view to presenting the detail to The Boss in the autumn. And in the coming week, before Frau Sturzenegger and the Sailing House open *Dubai Now* in Freiburg, we shall announce our collaboration to the German media. No desperate need to worry about word getting out before then, as even now little local news gets noticed by the Western media.

25 June

In Berlin, the young Polish girl at reception calls my attention to the fact that they will be screening *the game* in the upstairs lobby. To her incredulity, I ask who's playing whom at what. In an offended tone she tells me Germany is up against Turkey. She probably thinks I'm pulling her leg.

Five hours later the crowds are on the rampage outside the hotel. The street is cordoned off to control the groups of opposing German and Turkish fans trying to get past one another from opposite directions, brandishing flags and bottles. Germany lost, but make it to the finals anyway – victory of a kind. A win-win situation, perhaps?

28 June

The press conference on the lower level of the Mies van der Rohe building is well attended. I return to the city that branded me a traitor to the arts, as a government employee of the most ambitious metropolis in the Gulf. The host even sticks his neck out with mention of the United German Museums idea. If that's not badly received, then, well …

Very few questions after the presentations; individual interviews instead. Journalists in Germany prefer not to air their questions in public. But the tough ones I expected about finance, conditions for construction workers or freedom of expression don't come up in face-to-face discussions either.

I received a text message from Salem during the press conference. Apprehensive, I call him as soon as we've finished the final interview with a young woman from a local broadcaster in Munich who asks what it is about Bavaria that holds such attraction for Emiratis. Salem wants to know whether Sheikh Majed should attend the exhibition opening in Freiburg in national dress or in a Western suit. Why not in a *dishdash*? Salem is doubtful. Might not Western journalists take that as a sign of backwardness? I'm inclined to rule out such a possibility on the grounds that such prejudice would be a sign of backwardness in itself. But I wouldn't want to be answerable for German journalists.

30 June

The tough questions appear in the papers this morning. It is easier, after all, to posit answers to unasked questions if the object is merely to propound one's deeply sceptical view of the project. Opinion appears to be divided, though. The German review sections are unsure about what to make of this sudden interest in the Middle East and assume it must have something to do with raking in money. In Dubai, the project was announced on the real estate pages (there are no review pages to speak of as yet).

That evening there is a dinner at the invitation of a German–Emirati society I have never heard of. No one is introduced as the society's official representative. Around sixty people are seated in the salon of a downtown luxury hotel: a few grandees of the Berlin cultural scene, diplomats (mostly Eastern European) and parliamentarians. The Emiratis are well disguised but I meet the ambassador and his wife, who are very gracious and whose appearance here is noteworthy for the simple reason that they attend it together as a couple. Oddly, there is a Turkish band from Berlin's Moabit district playing away. There are no speeches.

The mystery of who is behind the society remains unsolved. The Arabs sit at tables near the entrance; the Westerners take seats by the windows. They do not mingle, with the exception of a Syrian woman who evidently lives in the city and is co-opted to entertain on such occasions. The absence of alcohol does nothing to lighten the atmosphere. The hors d'oeuvre leftovers have barely been carried away when people become uneasy, especially in the back section of the salon, and one by one they sneak away for about fifteen minutes at a time. To down a drink in the hotel bar, the neighbouring guest on my table suggests.

Here, in this superficially relaxed setting, people's real opinions finally get an airing. The editor on my left cannot conceive how I could possibly live in such a country. He once spent forty-eight hours in a nearby Emirate at its art biennial, which was forty-eight hours too long given the treatment of women and Asians there. I discover later that the directors of the biennial entertained him for two days in expectation of a favourable report in his newspaper on art exchange with the Middle East. I tell him I understand his position, but ask him to bear in mind that social conditions are not set in stone and that in my view it was important to make some attempt at least to demonstrate other values and ways of being in the world, with arts projects as much as anything else. What is culture for if not for exchange and dialogue? Someone eavesdropping behind me can contain himself no longer and asserts it's all about money. He found it hard to stomach the hypocrisy with which we spoke today, going on about culture at the press conference when what we really meant was money. The French were absolutely right to protest against the Louvre deal six months ago. It all points to a selling out of Europe.

This evening it looks as though a win-win situation might easily yield a lose-lose result.

Henry, Deira's general planner at Al Adheem, is dead. He collapsed in his office in one of the prefabricated barracks on the Creek. Cause of death: heart attack. The man was forty-four. That evening I receive an email from Azad inviting me to the funeral tomorrow afternoon, at a church in Jebel Ali. Henry's wife is being flown in from Melbourne to deal with the formalities of repatriating his not insubstantial remains.

7

3 July

I reach Freiburg in the afternoon. The Gysin Collection is housed in a 19th-century town house in a side alley in the town centre, not far from the train station. The exterior of this former middle-class home gives little impression of being a temple to art, apart from the poster hanging on the façade with a photograph by artist Reem Al Ghaith showing a veiled woman (with her back to the camera) standing before an endlessly ascending staircase. The woman's shadow seems very forlorn, and I imagine the image might strike a chord with many an Emirati. Several artists are waiting inside, the women in *abaya*s, the men mostly in jeans and tee shirts. They're happy to see a friendly face; I'm happy to see them too and shake hands warmly with the men.

The gallery has organized this show more or less by itself. We have funded the catalogue and the artists' flights, as well as the production of the artwork – videos and photos in the main. Sheikh Majed, the ruler's son and president of the Cultural Council, will open the show tomorrow.

Frau Sturzenegger and her team (of one? All I can see is a zippy young girl from Baden in a quirky hat) seem to have put up everything they could lay their hands on. The small exhibition rooms range over three floors and the permanent collection leaves us with little in the way of space. But the photos by Reem and other artists are mounted on large canvas flats and on the floor is a piece composed of stones wrapped in seaman's rope with tin cans and work boots, as well as sculptures made of flip-flops and toothbrushes. Space has also been found for a series of pictures portraying abandoned villas, and Frau Sturzenegger has set up a booth for viewing video installations in the stairwell, one showing an Emirati man in a *dishdash* toppling from a fishing boat into the sea. Over the whole exhibition hangs a pall of isolation, a kind of black-and-white loneliness.

Reem Al Ghaith is a shy art student in her early twenties whose opening gambit is to introduce her brother. Abdul-Hamid of the Sailing House fills me in later, telling me that Reem flew here in the family aircraft and will have to leave directly after the opening, because the family insists upon it and, in any case, she has a university exam the day after tomorrow. The mood is buoyant, despite none of us knowing what the outcome of this venture might be. Various television crews have expressed interest in reporting the event, and everyone seems to be anticipating the arrival tomorrow of the young sheikh. An exclusive reception on the roof terrace is planned that same evening for VIP guests.

4 July

The *Dubai Now* opening is set for 5 o'clock. Frau Sturzenegger, artists, journalists and guests gather in front of the Gysin Collection house. Among them is the head of the city's Culture Department, a representative from the German Ministry of Foreign Affairs in Berlin, and various other museum types from the wider vicinity. I spot Bouman there too, who waves from a distance, cellphone to his ear, stalking through the crowd on his long legs with his stooped torso, like a heron on the lookout for frogs in a bog. Half an hour or so later Salem sends me a text alerting me to difficulties. Sheikh Majed and his motorcade of black Daimler limousines have been stopped at the border on the way from the airport. Which border? Not knowing any better, the delegation had flown to Basel in

Switzerland, and their latter-day caravan has aroused suspicion on the German side at the border crossing in Weil. Sheikh Majed's passport has been mislaid and in the initial confusion no one can say what happened to it after it was inspected at the airport. I consider driving to the border and involving the man from the Ministry of Foreign Affairs.

But then everything is sorted out. The caravan shows up a good half-hour later. Frau Sturzenegger rolls out the red carpet at the last minute. There must be at least a hundred and fifty people from the culture and politics sectors looking on as Sheikh Majed and his thirty or so young escorts step from the nine vehicles and approach the red carpet with measured steps and solemn expressions. They all look the same: dark blue suits, black hair, black beards, all about the same age. So they decided against the *dishdash* after all. I take this as my cue and approach Sheikh Majed. His face lights up for a moment as he offers his hand and I extend a welcome, introducing Frau Sturzenegger (the collector himself is not present), Abdul-Hamid and the artists.

Majed is doubtless used to public appearances, though possibly not abroad. And this must be the first time he has opened an art exhibition – which is probably why he quickly reverts to his default air of solemnity. He rolls his shoulders like a gymnast every once in a while like he did at our first meeting, this time even while walking. The crowd edges closer, cameras flash, TV crews train their lenses on us, including an Emirati crew that has travelled here as part of the Sheikh's entourage. The artists wait by their pictures and installations for Sheikh Majed to view them. Someone has briefed them to explain the nature of their work and the young sheikh pays attention to a loyal subject of his own age as she explains her interest in the interiors of abandoned and neglected villas at home in the Gulf. The artists take the whole show in their stride with no visible sign of nerves, doubtless taking their lead from Abdul-Hamid. Sheikh Majed speaks in his familiar staccato manner and it's impossible to tell what he thinks of the exhibition. There are photos here showing Indian construction workers and the grubby side streets of Bur Dubai. It's not the glossy face of tourism the marketing men promote.

Suddenly, two older gentlemen appear in Majed's entourage who have neither introduced themselves to me nor travelled in the cars with the others. They too look strangely similar, even though they do not wear matching suits. Perhaps it's something to do with their wordless, tight-lipped demeanour. They move in closer to Majed, shielding him with their bodies. Abdul-Hamid looks very nervous but at the same time curiously satisfied.

A good hour later, the limousines roll out of Freiburg in the direction of the airport. Majed has received orders from home to travel back that same evening; the plane is needed tomorrow for another flight. Before leaving, he acquiesces in a group picture with his retinue, the artists and Frau Sturzenegger and says his farewells to all with a gentle wave and nod of his head. The two inscrutable and unidentified Arabs make their way back to the train station on foot, still without a word. As we approach Sheikh Majed's car to see him off, it starts to rain and one of his minders snaps open an umbrella. But Majed waves it away and turns to me to say that this is a sign of blessing where he comes from. Then the same is probably true here, I say.

No sooner has His Highness driven away than Frau Sturzenegger touches me lightly on the arm and whispers that there's something she needs to speak to me about. As she glances around to check no one is looking, I am taken aback by the downcast expression on her face, flushed though it still is with the success of the event. She wants to keep the Sailing House people from getting wind of something and leads me to her tiny office with its small, tidy desk with its solitary figurine of a cow beneath a Swiss cross. We sit down at an over-size conference table and Frau Sturzenegger embarks, with some hesitation, on the tale of woe that the *Muslim Faces* project has so far been. And it has nothing to do with tiresome conflicts with the owners of the lobby where the exhibition is to take place, or with the consul-general's strides being too long when he paced the measurements. It transpires that the Gysin Collection has yet to see a cent of the money it's owed. According to the contract, the first payment was due six weeks ago. If the money does not arrive in the next few days, things will be serious for the Collection with its small annual budget.

Nor is that all. Latifa has voiced serious misgivings about the Arabic translation of the catalogue – five weeks after receiving the text. Frau Sturzenegger reproaches herself for leaving the "young girl" alone with such a tricky task, though I wouldn't blame her for laying the responsibility on me. Latifa is apparently at loggerheads with the Iraqi translator commissioned by the publisher producing the catalogue. The Prophet, for instance, has not been dignified with all his attributes (The First and the Last, The Enlightened, Peace and Blessings upon Him …), and there are issues with other phrases besides. Latifa has informed the translator – but not me – that the text, as it stands, is completely unacceptable. The translator, who has worked with this publisher for years, argues that, as is common knowledge with Arabic, there are various ways of interpreting the material but there is not a single sentence in the catalogue that could be considered a breach of Sunni norms. Time is running out – in fact the print deadline was last week. If the translation isn't approved in three days, Frau Sturzenegger cannot guarantee that the catalogue will be ready and with us by the time the exhibition opens in early September.

Frau Sturzenegger has no need to mention Uzbekistan again. This experience has surpassed that. I stand, cast a helpless look down at the miniature cow, and squeeze the woman's hand longer than is customary before disappearing through the back door so no one will see me.

10 July

On the flight back I catch up with the press coverage of the exhibition opening – predictable sniping for the most part, making much of Gulf princes, and ritzy limousines, and obscenely rich collectors with "Zurich licence plates" at the evening reception, and the exhibitionist cheerleaders of the international art market drawn by the hype and exclusivity of the "art market's new Eldorado", rather than by a desire to view the artists' work on its own merits. Shy Emirati artists are accused of being defensive about their work in the face of attention from their own media broadcasting to a baffled home audience, in the presence of an equally diffident prince and his gawky entourage of apprentice courtiers.

The whole thing is written off as a propaganda exercise by the ruler, an attempt to convince a cultured and critical international audience that Emirati art is free of paternalism and as contemporary as the art in any Western country.

I am nonetheless convinced that the effort made by the Sailing House and the Gysin Collection was worth it. Many inquisitive and important people attended the opening, whatever their reasons. The fact that one paper labels me master of ceremonies for a modern dictatorship merely reinforces my opinion of that paper. But I'm annoyed at myself for letting it all get to me.

More importantly, I wonder how the thing has been received in the Gulf – and whether I'll ever find out.

I make a stopover in Beirut. Curiously, a fine trace of fresh blood on the stone floor by passport control grabs my attention. The airport is adorned with illuminated advertisements selling new arrivals the dream of their own house in paradise on an artificial island in the Gulf, just a three-hour flight from here.

Right now, there's a lull in hostilities; a fragile peace that for three decades has brought sporadic respite to Beirut's exhausted soul. The city displays its ruins with unabashed (or helpless) openness. The skeleton of the former Holiday Inn looms opposite the Phoenicia Hotel, reopened four years ago. The hotel was a battlefield during the Lebanese civil war and the bullet holes from the street fighting are in grisly evidence all about, sometimes sprayed with geometric precision on the concrete skins of the buildings, the graffiti of a conflict that knows neither beginning nor end, merely interruption. Grenades have left holes a storey high in some buildings and

Palestinian refugees sheltered in the burnt-out ruins up until a few years ago. This very area saw renewed gunfighting in the streets as recently as eight weeks ago.

It's a five-minute walk from the hotel to a beach club where a happy few frolic to the merciless pounding of house music: girls in tiny turquoise-and-cream-patterned bikinis straight out of *Vogue*, splashing in pools and sipping cocktails, watched by guys whose shoulder and back muscles are so pumped up they look physically deformed. In the summer ceasefire they can unleash their lust for life and enjoyment. Viewed from a deck leading to the pool, it's a cycle-of-life picture of Beirut today – youthful desire for abandon in the foreground, the gun-ravaged facades of the war behind; a backdrop for the last dance before the planes return. No wonder the faded beauties of Lebanon, women of a certain age, remind me of characters from a Chekhov play – it's the world-weariness of voice and gesture, the yearning without any real conviction of hope.

I attend a music festival in the President's summer palace in the mountains, an hour's drive from the city. The journey takes me through a landscape of hill-top villages reminiscent of Tuscany, past scores of military roadblocks. Before the concert I sit with Christina, a local theatre producer, on the terrace of the nearby hotel. We talk about the possibility of holding a similar festival in our city. A few minutes later she nods her head in the direction of the people at a neighbouring table. Apparently the man who has just taken a seat there is a minister. She says, with startling seriousness, that it would be best for us to settle up now and leave. Nothing here is as dangerous as being near a VIP. With few exceptions, the famous or notorious are avoided in public. Thus does prominence heighten the danger of assassination.

19 July

It's like being in the military; leaping out of bed and into the shower, out of the apartment and into the car, a nifty manoeuvre into the gap in the five-lane stop-go traffic, round the basement car park of the

Emirates Towers and into a space. The shortest path from car to lift is up a side staircase, past the guards and shopfronts with advertising posters of white bright young things leaning over a half-full glass of coloured liquid on the beach, smiling and wearing sporty sunglasses. Hundreds of pinstriped lieutenants from Europe, Arabia and India stream through the corridors from all directions, on their way to offices with briefcases, laptops and coffee cups in their hands, early morning smiles on their faces, the marble floor echoing beneath their feet. Up and away (to the 21st floor in my case) with computer switched on and booted and new emails retrieved. Something approaching forty have come in since I last checked before my departure yesterday evening.

Then the server goes down and I can't answer any of them. Forward march, halt! The staff drift in, Carmen then Latifa and Khalil, the morning sun winking through the narrow windows. I need to be on the phone now with China, with Salem, with The Boss, with the German consul-general. But most of all I need to go to the beach, to the little fishing harbour in Jumeirah, where bleary-eyed Pakistani fishermen, who returned a few hours ago at dawn with the catch they've now sold to Deira merchants, are lying down in *barasti* huts or sheds of plywood and cardboard for a few hours' rest, before they inspect the nets for the evening run and tuck into slow-cooked curries and rice.

In the Emirates Tower, we can only dream of such productivity. There is no news about progress on Khor Dubai. There is no more talk of a Director-General. It might be the Emiratis have no problem with this stagnation. Everything whizzes around them but they remain calm and serene, happy to let things whirl. I should have realized long ago that in a system like this one can perform no better than the people on whom one depends. If the supervisor is a failure, his subordinate, no matter how hard he pushes himself, will end up a failure too – a friendlier failure perhaps, more efficient, more reliable, but a failure none the less.

To my mind, the problem here is not so much the lack of freedom to create, but the hierarchy. It's an absolute monarchy but with nothing so simple as one person ruling absolutely; rather it's an uncontrolled, shifting power base within a royal household. No one seems to have the *final* word.

Try putting a decision into effect unilaterally and you stand a good chance of making yourself look ridiculous in the eyes of your colleagues and everyone else. The consensus of one's superiors is vital. Loss of face is a basic fear and people go to great lengths of inventiveness to avoid it. Authority conferred is used not so much to take action, but to cultivate personal image and enhance status.

Latifa takes a seat at my desk and delivers two pieces of good news: the government's financial accounts department has just confirmed the transfer of the Gysin Collection funds, and the catalogue foreword she drafted for The Boss was approved by his office this morning. But her main concern is to discuss her misgivings about the translation. She also insists on my opinion regarding her choice of a new Gucci *abaya*. I know we have to take her concerns seriously.

Her instincts are in a sense those of the collective. If she has objections, other people will have them too. I promise her that I will send Frau Sturzenegger an email as soon as the server is up and running.

22 July
A letter from the director of a gallery in Manhattan's Chelsea district, expressing an interest in including the *Dubai Now* exhibition in its autumn programme. The Salone di Milano too is inviting our participation this coming season and there are similar inquiries from festival organizers and art centres in Lisbon, Paris, Hong Kong and Rotterdam. Abdul-Hamid and Frau Sturzenegger have accomplished an unexpected triumph for the city and its Cultural Council. We shall of course need a little more money, perhaps as much as for Freiburg, to travel to New York with *Dubai Now*. By the autumn! Frau Sturzenegger has promised to take on the organization.

But can Salem present this in clear terms to The Boss? Rather than answer the question on the telephone, Salem appears in my office. The exhibition is complicated, he says. I enquire what he means by that. He looks at me as though he wishes I hadn't asked. There could be almost no better reaction to the exhibition, I add. Abdul-Hamid has been giving interviews, Salem breaks in. Did I know about it? An image pops into my mind of the two Arabs who appeared from nowhere in Majed's entourage and disappeared without trace! For once I see Salem with furrowed brow. We've got to stop playing the victim, he says – a phrase he has clearly picked up from someone else. Abdul-Hamid, reportedly, has been telling international journalists that Emirati artists face censorship. We must not provide opportunities to feed Western prejudices, he says. I argue that Abdul-Hamid isn't saying anything new by that and by issuing statements to the contrary we would undermine his credibility. The exhibition contains too many no-go photos, Salem interjects. So that means they can't be shown in other places? Does this mean we have to cut the Freiburg show short? Salem shakes his head slowly. No, the exhibition stays where it is. But no other cities for now. Perhaps we should show it here. I ask him if he's serious. If it were up to him, that's what he'd do.

24 July

Temperatures of forty-nine degrees were recorded in Al Ain yesterday. The heat is leaching the colour from the facades of villas, from cars and from the landscaped green areas around the Tower. A bleached-out cityscape devoid of people. Even the most stony-hearted developers have to cut back on the working hours.

It looks as if tidy-up season has been called at The Boss' office. All sorts of interesting things are surfacing. The Sheikh Mansour project, for example (or "projects" if you include the pilfered Pavilion). I answer an email enquiry about this from the office manager as briefly as possible: until the Khor Dubai development is signed off, this project cannot be assessed. We need the expertise of professional building contractors. I don't bother mentioning that I've already explained all this, two months ago now.

The query reminds me we have a board of directors. Whatever happened to Matthieu and Banderas? Or to Mansour himself, come to that?

27 July

A summer break is out of the question. Every day, a steady flow of enquiries about various pending projects trickles down to our office from the 52nd floor. Salem has taken to describing himself as a volcano on the verge of erupting.

Behula, the office manager, is blithely diverting to us an assortment of people whose appointments with The Boss have been in the diary for months.

Ours is the pleasure of receiving two staff-members of a natural history museum in Dallas. An American Asian named Lee does all the talking. Lee has pomaded hair, shiny pinkish skin and a gleaming grin. He has left his jacket in the car and his red-and-white-striped braces are on full display over his crisp, white shirt. Having seen *Destiny in the Desert*, I now know this is the look that boxing referees cultivate.

"Hello friends!" he trills to Latifa, Salem, Tarek and me as we await his presentation in the conference room. "What an amazing opportunity this is to introduce you to our *unique* museum. You know of course that there are many natural history museums in the world. But *we* are one of a kind! We don't want to waste your time with hazy concepts! Make no mistake about it: The Humble NatHist in Dallas is the most lucrative and successful museum of its kind in the world. We have the greatest number of visitors …" He pauses. "The highest profit …" He pauses again. "The most modern exhibition … aaaand …" – he stretches the vowel and leaves the word hanging before continuing – "we don't need donations. We finance ourselves. How do we do it, you ask? Listen up!"

He fires up a PowerPoint presentation with a map of the United States, that zooms in on a satellite map of Texas, then Dallas and finally down to the Humble NatHist. Figures and tables follow, demonstrating a world-beating position in comparison with New York, London, Paris and so on. "First there were the Europeans," says Lee, "yesterday the East Coast of the United States, and today it's our turn." By his reckoning, in Europe it's the day before yesterday. So Dallas beats them all, in terms of visitors, profit and square metres too. Especially square metres, because the Humble NatHist is not actually a museum. It's a theme park – with plenty of space for Texan shoppers to play, amid the Neanderthals and the dinosaurs.

Right after the statistics, Lee forges ahead with "Vision Dubai". Under no circumstances will he allow us a glimpse of his Texan museum exhibits or the finds from its archaeological digs. There is to be no deviation from his remotely controlled path of learning that will lead to the virtual enlightenment of the Gulf population. He has a Humble NatHist of Dubai in mind. Dubai is to become a second Dallas. Remote control in his left hand, right thumb tucked under the strap of his braces, it's full speed ahead into the future of revealing the past. The Humble NatHist Dubai is a little speck of desert with a 250,000-square-metre surface area (just about twice that of the Louvre, if I remember correctly), which will be transformed into a natural history park. Lee rubs his hands and leads us over primeval volcanoes and Pleistocene glaciers. Herds of dinosaurs hunt above our heads, we drift past gigantic, antediluvian fish, climb the skeleton of a *Brachiosaurus brancai* that narrates, in a Texan accent, how it made its way to the deserts of the Gulf. "You guys ever seen anything like it?" Well, of course not.

I glance over at my Emirati colleagues and Latifa shoots me an ironic grin. Lee has come to his pièce de résistance: a globe about twenty metres in diameter hanging from the ceiling of a custom-made pavilion – the centrepiece of the Humble NatHist Dubai. Other than this, everything else we've seen might also be found in Dallas. But the globe, developed in co-operation with NASA and Google, is on offer to us, exclusively – the world in a twenty-metre Google nutshell. Surrounding it are galleries with monitors installed. These monitors work like microscopes. The visitor touches the surface of the screen and zooms into his favourite fishing spot in the Rockies, measures the water temperature on the beach of Franz Josef Land or checks to see that no one is illicitly cavorting in his garden. Lee demonstrates how you zoom in on these topographical details, with a little set of exercises he performs from left to right of the screen and back again.

It looks like Google Earth to me. "You can look down on your own head," says Lee. "We can already do that now, on the computer," Tarek interjects. "Yes but this here is three-dimensional, boys!" A pedant would have to correct him on this point but Lee is no doubt a true believer in the three-dimensional. Meanwhile, he's moved on to the weather observation station: "Who has the biggest carbon footprint?" Lee notices too late that this is possibly not his best idea, as the Gulf region pops up on screen. "OK," he says, "you guys will get that under control soon enough. But look: who has the biggest oil reserves?" The Arabian Peninsula appears once again. Lee is now shiny all over; even his braces it seems are aglow.

A portrait of the ruler appears on his last slide. Our boxing referee wants to demonstrate just how much he knows about the city, His Highness and his vision. He quotes strategy papers, quotes quotes, and everything he says points conclusively to the Humble NatHist Dubai. Have we talked about the cost? But Lee has to pass on this one. The globe is estimated at one hundred million (dollars? dirhams? He doesn't specify). Impossible to arrive at a meaningful calculation, he says, without an in-depth analysis and the appropriate market research as well as an investigation of real estate considerations. Naturally, the Humble NatHist team can be commissioned to undertake such work at any time.

An hour and fifteen minutes later we're finished. Salem thanks Lee for his time and assures him that he has not wasted ours. To my relief, I note that Salem has judged my mood accurately and takes the matter into his own hands. He promises Lee that Tarek will be in touch with him "very soon".

28 July

I don't know if it's just a coincidence but today we are treated to a visit from Lee's London competitor. So London is living in the day before yesterday, is it? I would love to put the question to Lee, but the rules of commercial confidentiality prohibit me from revealing anything about this approach from his rival. The jury's out as to whose presentation is better but the contrast in attitude is certainly apparent. Our pleasure in this performance is akin to the kind one gets from watching a peep show: as the Brits do their stuff I am struck less by what they are presenting than by the way they do it. They too present us with a gargantuan globe, developed in co-operation with NASA and Google, but they make no claim for it having been developed exclusively for us. There's undoubtedly a difference in mentality between Today's offering and the Day before Yesterday's.

Just to keep our spirits up, Salem introduces a proposal for a Museum of the Future – from the US of course. The Chinese have not yet

reached the point of wanting to show the future in a museum. At a time of disenchantment with the reality of the East German communist vision, the dramatist Heiner Müller posed the question: *Where today is that tomorrow I saw yesterday?* It's a question that touches a particular nerve just now.

This selfless philanthropic proposal comes from a director of the Hollywood Shooting Stars production company, who showed one of his productions at the film festival here in December and seized the opportunity to acquaint local movers and shakers with other talents and business interests of his that extend far beyond the realm of the film business.

A work group had been convened on the 52nd floor to assume responsibility for developing this promising, if singular, project. The group appears to have come to the conclusion that foolproof implementation of a Museum of the Future from LA requires professional help from one of the three biggest consulting companies in the world – known for their experience of global business, economics and politics, though not at all for their expertise in the cultural sphere, and who conveniently have about a hundred foot-soldiers employed here already. And, a few months and doubtless hundreds of thousands of consulting dollars later, somebody in The Boss's office appears to have remembered us. Winston was probably too busy to deal with it and Behula has possibly happened upon the yellowing press release on Khor Dubai and the Cultural Council during her marathon clean-up.

I take a good look at the documentation. Our Hollywood phil-anthropist has had some doodles drawn – easy on the eye as far as the iconic dildo-style architecture goes; a futuristic flight of fancy in a bubble spanning at least 150,000 square metres and housing entertainment technology on the theme of basic cultural needs such as food, shelter, locomotion, shopping and sleeping. It looks as if the content of this bubble has been conceived by the man of the moment – Mr Disney himself.

The cost of the whole thing (to the proprietors) is said to be almost nothing. The 200-million-dollar investment is peanuts by local standards and, according to estimates by the experts called in, will be recouped in the blink of an eye. Allegedly Bill Gates and Steve Jobs, Al Gore and the project's initiator have already hinted at their participation. What could possibly go wrong? How could anyone object that two million visitors at an average entrance fee of 30 dollars a head might be an over-estimate? Or the area too big? Or the lack of conceptual work glaringly obvious? Or that one or two firm and final partners for the development (as well as Al Gore of course) might be desirable?

All of this is just pessimism from the Day before Yesterday, I tell myself that evening as I'm feeding the turtles. The female gorges on so much raw ham that all she can do is loll under a floating plastic island as the male, only half her size, takes his turn. I have named him Europa but I am quite incapable of coming up with a name for his female counterpart. I've tried Oprah, Armada and Landslide, but none of them has stuck.

Pictures of the American presidential candidate Obama in Berlin on TV. There's no escaping him. You see him everywhere, even here

in the Gulf. The more I'm forced to look at a face, the more enervating its effect on me. I expect he's the right man for America. Not that anyone there is interested in my opinion.

Does anyone here give a fig for my opinion about anything? Does the Cultural Council? When it comes to a Museum of the Future, for example? I doubt it. They love the idea on the 52nd floor and I expect it has little to do with the concept, because so far there isn't one to speak of. They are flattered that the man from Hollywood, and by extension America, thought of us at all. America is the land of Today and, if the TV screen is anything to go by, perhaps even the land of Tomorrow.

So The Boss, in his enthusiasm for this Hollywood attention, brought the consulting firm on board and they've assigned a load of inexperienced Turkish talent to the project to work on what amounts to the production of benevolent platitudes. Now we have a Future Museum Dubai. At least in theory. Ride the right magic horse in this city and with luck you'll make it up to the 52nd floor on your first jump. Which is why no museum has been built here for a long time.

But at least you can get a buzz going. It is no coincidence that the horses usually emanate from the land of boundless possibilities. By his own account, the ruler breeds his own horses there too. Here you might not love Americans, but you almost definitely find them uniquely visionary.

29 July

A Muslim Indian from the Johannesburg area takes a seat next to me on the flight to Amman. His wife sits on his other side. They are both in their sixties. The woman neither looks at me nor says anything. His complexion has, I like to think, an Indian Ocean quality, and he has a long nose and staring, close-set eyes. About an hour into the flight we chat a bit. They're on their way to Jerusalem. I tell him it isn't safe there right now. He tells me it's not really a problem for Europeans. An interesting thought, that: suicide bombers only target Muslims. As he sees it, the danger of terrorist attacks issues only from the Israelis.

I'm in Jordan at the invitation of the *Cityscape Middle East* real estate trade fair where I'm to give a lecture on Khor Dubai. Hope springs eternal, so my presentation is an attempt to give voice to the aspirations of our headless Cultural Council, before an audience permeated by a kind of bigoted cultural indifference. One introduces projects likely to have long disappeared into drawers or waste-baskets. Sometimes you know it, sometimes you don't. Sometimes even the others know it. But usually no one cares. No one raises any objection to a property development business where architecture plays the prostitute to investors. They simply do business instead. Nevertheless I have a little attack prepared. Khor Dubai as a *concept*-grounded project with Shakespeare's *Coriolanus* to back me up: "What is the city but the people?" "True, the people are the city." Not its architecture.

The taxi driver enquires whether Daimler cars are as expensive in Dubai as they are here. I actually do see several 1980s models with the "D" country indicator on the way from the airport to the capital, but with Jordanian licence plates. Twenty years ago in Germany such vehicles were known as Turkish Mercedes or Turkish janitor Mercedes. Not even the junkyards in Dubai would take these models these days.

We draw closer to the city, originally built on seven hills but now spanning nineteen. Amman inhabits the landscape like a meandering labyrinth of sprawling sandstone-coloured honeycombs, a naked city on a friable land surface. On the face of it, it is a recent city built almost entirely during the latter half of the 20th century. Unlike its neighbours, Jerusalem and Damascus, Amman has had an inter-rupted history of settlement. Yet the citadel with its Umayyad palace, Roman amphitheatre and Byzantine church point to its antiquity, reaching back to Canaanite times. They say the royal family, the Hashemites of Meccan origin, is descended directly from the Prophet. Eighty-five percent of all inhabitants are Palestinian, Iraqi, Kuwaiti and Syrian. It is the biggest refugee camp for every war that has taken place in the region. Maybe that's why it feels so gentle and sleepy. Even the security forces checking the front of the hotel for weapons or explosives look to me as though they're collecting donations for a relief organization.

There are more live cats at the market than dead meat and poultry for sale. It smells of tobacco, caraway and engine oil. Booths are covered with tarpaulin as protection against the sun, merchants linger in the shadows, and only once in a while does one of them call out an offer over the quietly milling crowd. Building facades sport cracks the width of a hand; many windows are boarded up with plywood or covered with carpets. Pigeons fill the skies above the alleys. *Cityscape*. On the way here I read in an in-flight magazine how this open area known as "Downtown" Amman will look in a few years: glass and steel shops fronting onto marble terraces with bubbling fountains; malls with strolling, faceless consumers. The advertisement might just as easily be promoting one of the real estate projects in the Gulf. The question is, who can afford this rubbish and who would want to pay for it?

To my surprise, I run into Banderas and Sheikh Mansour in the hotel lobby. They've obviously just had lunch together and are bidding each other farewell. The sheikh is on his way to the courtyard and is in a hurry. He shakes my hand brusquely, barely looking at me, asks how I am doing and, as he rushes off, growls that we'll certainly be seeing each other soon in Dubai. Banderas squares up to me and tells me how peeved he is at being excluded from our work. I nod, hoping to give the impression that not only do I understand his resentment but share it, and quickly steer the conversation to the reason for his stay in Amman.

As expected, this loosens him up. He will be giving a *lecture* today in a large auditorium at the university. People love him here. For weeks his website has been flooded by mail from Jordanian fans looking forward to the event. Then, hardly able to believe my eyes, I spot Winston approaching. I recognize him by his walk. Semi-circling the master, he whisks a hardback edition of Banderas's new book from his briefcase, and begs him for an autograph for his daughter. She has read *everything* by him. Winston is the man to make Banderas happy. The master asks for the name and age of the daughter and scrawls his dedication in large letters on the title page. Winston peers over his shoulder like a little boy as he writes. The sage returns the book, bids me an abrupt goodbye and takes his leave.

Winston has already turned to leave when he asks over his shoulder how things are going. But he's in too much of a hurry for my explanation about the *Cityscape* presentation. He's busy doing the rounds of the region's significant festivals and conferences. Networking. The way he says it, it sounds a bit like "not working". I grant him a curt nod.

Touitou and Zold vouchsafe us a glimpse of their genius with their entries in a competition for projects in the Arab world. In essence, their presentations boil down to those little films that lay audiences find at once impressive and intimidating, opening with a bird's-eye view of a city and zooming down like an eagle onto the construction site. Rendering after rendering, introducing ever more audacious constructions in ever more improbable shapes – high-gloss cartoons that cock a snook at the natural laws of physics.

In between there are panel discussions in which participants demonstrate their knowledge of the country in which they've newly touched down by sprinkling their conversation with facts hastily gleaned from a mile-high google search on the intercontinental flight here. Types like these usually seek to sugar their one-size-fits-all ideas by ingratiating themselves with their attentive audience – expressions of admiration for local attempts at modernization usually do the trick.

An American, well-known for his global ambitions when it comes to franchising his brand of museum, takes the routine a little too far. He mixes three-year-old PowerPoint slides of his toy museums in Europe and Asia with photos showing Hollywood greats on motorcycles in the desert. "We're not Bilbao," someone in the audience shouts, "We were around even before you!" But the man from New York wouldn't be what he is if he had no answer to that: "What do you mean by Westernization?" he asks. "Frank Lloyd Wright developed a plan for a museum in Baghdad in the 1950s and paved the way for Arab modernity!" There is strong evidence to suggest that the time for a new Arab Modernism has come, he declares in sonorous tones. This dictum is apparently sufficient to quell further discussion. Thus subdued, the audience reverts to its air of uneasy gratitude.

My own contribution on Khor Dubai is cobbled together from concept proposals, historical material, day-to-day observation, anecdotes, reflections on misunderstandings, and a few bits of comparative data borrowed from Bouman.

I put up a slide showing iconic buildings designed in the last two years – banks, stadiums, and museums from all over the world, conceived in the offices of prize-winning architectural firms as famous as the buildings they've designed. Ostentatious designs recognizable as buildings only because of their familiarity in the media, are lined up on the slide, one luscious diva after the other. One can imagine speech bubbles emanating from them, each cutting its neighbour down to size. The next slide shows examples of work by unknown architects from the Arab world. The principle is the same, the effect similar to that of the celebrity architects. On the third slide is an assorted mix of the two. The conclusion is obvious. This isn't architecture; it's narcissism. These are not examples of beautiful form serving a useful purpose, they are monuments to the ambition and vanity of their creators.

I end with a plea for a culture of architecture without icons. The sentiment is a direct consequence of my current experiences (though I don't say as much).

Afterwards Touitou and Zold, who stood very close to me before my presentation, disappear with the other speakers. I don't feel particularly lonely, despite grasping that none of the invited experts has any desire to engage with me. Backs are turned to me. No doubt there will be a reception in the hotel around now. After an exhausting day in Amman, the speaking and debating contingents will mull over the pros and cons of this city, that is to say the quality of the hotels and taxi service and of course the upcoming projects and business prospects, and architectural competitions elsewhere. I'd better not go there.

Conference participants press business cards into my hand. I don't give out any of my own but promise to stay in touch – a precaution-ary measure. A local, middle-aged woman collars me and bends my ear about the proposed new theatre for Amman. The architect, she assures me, is Jordanian and he's supposed to be attending a dinner to which she is also invited. I end up in her 1981-model Mercedes, riding through the market district again, past the Roman theatre, through narrow alleyways and up the hill. We're standing in a park stuffed with sculptures, a few scattered cypresses between them stretching up to the clear night sky. It's a bit like a cemetery. Farther back is a large house, the door of which opens as we approach between the lanterns. The old gentleman waving at us is not the architect but Mamdouh, our host and the country's only duke. The woman told me the story on the way here: Mamdouh comes from an old family with enormous estates in the north, around the Golan, which were worthless until recently. He once found himself with the King at the onset of a sudden downpour and had the presence of mind to open an umbrella over His Majesty's head. The King is said to have asked his friend what he wanted in return for this service; Mamdouh asked for the title of duke.

The house is thronged with local artists and European and Arab diplomats. The architect is here too but is so intensely engaged in conversation with the French ambassador's wife that I manage only to shake his hand. In Mamdouh's abandoned library (with thousands of books in at least four languages), Signora Tebaldi sings Violetta like no one has before her or ever will again. No matter that the record is scratched and Violetta repeats the same phrase over and over. I take a seat on an old chaise longue and survey the pictures round the room: Mamdouh with King Hussein in a tuxedo, with King Hussein in a bomber jacket, with King Hussein in a *dishdash*. And Mamdouh with an assortment of blonde and dark-haired beauties. Violetta's dying notes settle like a glaze on the book-bindings, on the buzzing party voices from the salon and on the unanswered question hammering in my head: What the hell am I doing with my life? *Addio del passato* indeed.

30 July

With Hassidic Jews on the flight back. Royal Jordanian takes them to Dubai, for a connecting flight they will board without setting foot in the United Arab Emirates. For them, entry to an Arab country is as good as impossible and Amman is like the Tränenpalast or "Palace of Tears" – the Berlin station at the former border crossing where visiting citizens of the divided city bade farewell to relatives barred from travelling to the West of the city. This part of the world was once taboo for Israelis. Anyone wanting to travel to India, Japan, or China would first have to backtrack to Europe (to Rome or Athens, for instance) and take off from there. But for a few years now, Israelis have been able to catch a bus in Jerusalem or Tel Aviv for Jordan's Queen Alia Airport and fly east from here.

Yahweh's devotees are sitting in the row in front of me. They've kept their hats on over stringy, dark curls dangling from either side. Centred in the monitor above their heads is a pictogram of an aircraft with the cockpit towards the bottom. While we're in flight, an arrow and a black box move around the pictogram from seven to eleven o'clock, showing our position relative to the Kaaba in Mecca. I'm not sure what kind of mood the gentlemen in front of me are in. Maybe they're as apprehensive as my Aunt Lisbeth when she took the cross-border train from West Berlin through the DDR to Bebra thirty years ago. The feeling of arriving in Dubai must be even stranger for them. They're entering a territory and not entering it. Hovering in no man's land before another plane carries them off somewhere else.

31 July

The view from my apartment window over the bright glowing light of the highway and its chain of high-rises. The absence of life down there gives the illusion of being in a falcon's nest with a view of the whole world beneath. If that sounds grandiose, it's because it's meant to, and contemptuous, too. From up here you are treated to regular sight of the whole anomalous madness at work in this unpleasantly exclusive place. Unpleasant because, from this perspective, you see what one might call this global destination for what it is: a simulated city for the purpose of display, the only order, however makeshift, in this aggregation of concrete, asphalt, glass and steel being the verticals of the towers and the horizontals of the streets. The towers create the illusion of a margin, an interior space, a present reality of a city. But it doesn't hold. Beyond their short shadows, everything bleeds into an infinity of sand and sea, all parallels swallowed. This city's highways lead everywhere …

And nowhere. The illusion of urban mass is sustainable only at street level, from a frog's eye view. From up here it's another story, it's a peek behind the curtain to a desert void that receives with indifference this outpouring of the human imagination.

July

The more you gaze down into the city, the more the world gazes back at you. This window of mine presents a thousand panoramas. Today, it may seem there is nothing going on down below, but there is. There are people down there; in the streets, in their cars, in offices or in beds all over this city. In *every* city. If you listen hard enough you might hear in a pause between voices the howl of their longing, their greed and their grief.

There is no going back to the illusion of a sheltered home. I shall leave this city sooner or later; but its manifold gaze will follow me wherever I go.

8

I August

Yusuf, my Bedouin friend from the desert, calls to ask when the exhibition of "his people" is taking place. He means *Muslim Faces*. There's no getting it out of his head. He has to posses his soul in patience for another six weeks. It will open at the start of Ramadan. The main reason for his interest is Abdullah. The old man, Yusuf says, now lives in the Hajar Mountains, in a wadi near Hatta village, and he wants to see the faces of his forefathers one more time before he dies. Is Abdullah very ill? I enquire. No. Yusuf wants to know why I'm asking. I'm not sure if we understand each other; the mobile is distorting Yusuf's voice. Finally we hang up without having clarified the matter. I have noticed that the more traditional Emiratis do not like to talk about illness. In the wadis around Hatta are a few small, scrubby oases among the bare limestone mountains. In all likelihood Abdullah is sitting in a palm-shaded hut, stoically waiting for his time to come.

There are rumours that untreated sewage is being secretly and illegally dumped into Dubai's inland storm drain network and finding its way into the sea. Truck drivers who are paid by the lorry load to collect waste from the city's septic tanks face long delays and have to queue for up to twelve hours to unload at Dubai's only official sewage treatment plant, so some drivers are taking a shortcut and dumping

their loads after dark straight into manholes meant only for rain-water. The city authorities are reportedly incapable of tracking down the culprits. Conspiracy is ruled out. Even in swanky Jumeirah and Umm Suqeim, bulky plastic pipelines can be seen stretched across the beach to the water, spewing out grey balls of human waste.

Tourists adventurous enough to risk the blazing heat at this time of year have apparently received no warning to stay away from the water. There are still a few bathers bobbing about, utterly carefree, in the gently lapping waves.

2 August

One or two members of senior management at Al Adheem and Arab Properties have been arrested on suspicion of forgery and falsi-fication of documents, according to *The Emirates* newspaper. British and American newspapers speculate whether recent fraud and bribery investigations are a result of internal power struggles, or else a sign of Dubai's determination to send a clear message to the outside world that it is a clean and law-abiding place to do business. The possibility that it might be a simple case of corruption such as you might find in any other country of the world, seems not to have occurred to them. Even members of well-known local families stand among the accused.

3 August

Decide around midnight to take a walk on the beach. Ebb tide and stillness. The golden contours of a mosque glow in the darkness, the Sheikh Zayed Road skyline twinkles, unreal, beyond. Never felt lonelier. The long shirt, all I am wearing, sticks to my skin in the dampness. Osmosis on the Gulf – body perspiration mingling with ambient humidity. I walk slowly, feeling like a short-winded old man. The world contracts into a single, small, shameless wish: *Get me out of here.*

16 August

Mannheim, south-west Germany, for a Goethe Institute symposium, having jumped in at the last minute when a Syrian speaker withdrew. I'm here to say something about Khor Dubai and arrive minutes before my scheduled appearance in the early afternoon. I enter the conference hall as an Asian woman is giving an illustrated talk on catastrophe-hit jungle villages to an audience of about eight hundred people, most of them young. The moderator is a German woman in her thirties with one of those short, asymmetrical haircuts that leave a distracting strand of hair dangling over one eye. Without introducing herself she informs me that we will be starting soon and there has been a delay. Instead of the two hours previously allotted we're now down to just half that for the afternoon session. For this reason, there'll be no discussion between speakers, let alone any exchange with the audience.

Only at this point do I get first sight of the list of speakers on my panel: the former mayor of Accra, a woman from Rio involved with a cultural initiative, an expert in matters of population development from Mumbai, an Indonesian Secretary of State for Culture, and myself.

I don't exactly fit the profile of the people on this list. The African tells the story of how, after a flood a few months before, he had to pacify a furious woman by assuring her that he hoped to restore friendly relations with the river spirits by allowing the continued disposal of dead family members in the river. The man from Jakarta gives a report on pressure groups demanding more freedom of expression. The Brazilian is a member of a work group for the re-socialization of drug addicts.

In the course of my presentation, I am seized by the notion that the Ghanaian river gods might well be amusing themselves by casting a spell on the renderings, masterplans and skyscraper silhouettes depicted on my PowerPoint slides, morphing them magically into soulless monuments to the decadence of oil wealth. I try to concentrate but am careless enough to claim that, among other things, the Khor Dubai project aims to encourage new forms of multi-cultural expression. Such a purpose must surely be of interest to this international audience of so-called culture managers.

When my allotted time is up, I obediently take my seat next to the moderator who, instead of moving straight to the next speaker, tosses her head with a whiplash flick of her hair and expresses her regret that there is no time to discuss this dubious claim to multiculturalism. A glance at the latest Human Rights Watch report, for instance, shows how things stand with respect to the rights of thousands of construction workers. She is doubtful, personally, that the cultural needs of these and other silent minorities, who in truth constitute the majority of the population, will have been considered at all in this development.

This comment elicits a smattering of applause from the back rows, principally from a person in a black tee shirt and yellow baseball cap. The moderator's outspokenness rankles, particularly since I am given no right of reply to a rebuke that is not only public, but for which she seeks audience approval before moving swiftly on to the Indian academic, who springs to his feet and delivers his talk with a glassy expression.

When it's all over and the speakers have said their goodbyes, I can't resist asking her about her day job. Freelance journalist, she replies, with a hard stare, for daily newspapers and broadcasting corporations. That figures. It's the kind of behaviour I've come to expect from her profession in recent months, I say: a standard practice of delivering pat, rehearsed answers to questions that were never raised, for reasons of time. Only now does she want to debate with me the gross injustices she has read about in the Human Rights Watch report, but she doesn't get the chance because, in the meantime, the yellow baseball cap has worked his way to the front and is now squaring up to me. I should be glad there was no audience discussion, says he. "We would have eaten you alive." I ruminate pointlessly on who might be included in this collective threat and notice a group of young women standing nearby. Their body language does not, however, signal any immediate danger of violent action against the capitalist/imperialist inhumanity of the oil business, which is apparently embodied by me on this occasion.

One of the young women turns to speak to me, jolting me from my thoughts. Her name is Sunny and she's an Iranian who grew up in Stuttgart. Sunny tells me she studied International Cultural Management at university and would like to do an internship with us. Only half joking, I ask her if she really wants to take up with human rights violators. But Sunny is in deadly earnest. In her considered view the inequalities in the Gulf region only go to show how important it is to get involved and to build culture. I would like to pursue this with her in greater depth but propriety demands I exchange a few courtesies with the city council dignitary who has just descended upon us. So I slip her my business card and encourage her to get in touch, though sadly there are no internships planned at the moment.

The head of the city planning department witnessed the tussle in front of the podium and attempts an embarrassed apology. But I wave it away, and he seems relieved. He brings greetings from the mayor, escorts me to the foyer and presents me with a coffee-table book on the city of Mannheim. I am honoured and a little taken aback.

But there's no time to linger as I have a train to catch to the capital and so I flip through the book on the journey. The citizens of Mannheim are a cosmopolitan bunch of 160 nationalities. Though the grid-system layout of its "Mannheim squares" might be interpreted as the pure expression of feudal absolutism, it apparently inspired the plans for Washington DC. And at the end of the 17th century it was the first city in Germany, and possibly Europe, to appoint a foreign mayor. In other words, it nurtured not just Schiller, the poet of human brotherhood, but globalization too. Perhaps the two go hand in hand, it's just that too few Mannheimers have a sense of it. The book is lavishly illustrated with interesting photos and weighs quite a bit too. It's fortunate I didn't meet the departmental head first thing – I might have been tempted to hurl it at the protester's lemon-yellow cranium.

19 August

Berlin. A farewell send-off befitting a general – one of the three who came to Dubai. The invitation is also extended to the exotic partners in the Gulf. Manage to convince Salem to attend for a few hours at least, and discover in passing that he's just become engaged! I shall not, of course, be meeting his bride; or if I do it'll only be by chance as the two scurry past me in a shopping mall. Salem, at just under thirty, has left it a bit late by Emirati standards, I observe. He explains quite earnestly that he has had to fight a very personal 45-Day Syndrome over the years. After six weeks of smouldering love for a woman it goes cold, every time, leaving him no choice but to dissolve the relationship. But this time it's been three months and is still going strong. Everything is back on track, Emirati-style.

We have been advised that we need attend only the evening reception at the Neue Nationalgalerie. Several longer speeches are planned for the commemorative event itself in the early afternoon; which is a bit too much to expect of Salem. And a bit much for me, come to that. Nevertheless, I am curious enough to sneak into the Humboldt University auditorium shortly before noon. The hall is packed with elderly men in dark suits. At that moment the chairman of the friends' association refers to the general as the Arnold Schwarzenegger of German art, prompting sniggers and groans from the audience. Actually there is more nervous tension than sympathy evident on the faces of those present. Not sure if this has as much to do with the speaker as the general. It is not unusual on such occasions for suppressed resentments or disappointments to rear their heads. There's always the chance that, besides the employee who has always doubted the competence of his soon-to-be-ex boss, there's someone who may have been snubbed or wronged at some point. The chairman of the appreciation society finishes twenty minutes later and turns directly to the guest of honour, his face beaming. The honoured gentleman mounts the stage, visibly touched as he receives his gift from the chairman, handed to him by an assistant who is a renowned lawyer by profession. It's a large portfolio containing drawings and photographs by Berlin artists. The general is barely capable of speech, such is the lump in his throat.

That evening Salem and I arrive at the Nationalgalerie a good half-hour after the appointed time. We pass through the watergate, show our tickets and find a Jeff Koons exhibition on the ground floor while the party is in full swing downstairs. Though just now there's another speech being made. Since the stairs down are crammed with guests, Salem and I take a stroll between the garish Koons pieces arranged about the hall and wait for the end of the speeches. The exhibition, according to the handout, is a collection of spectacular productions from the artist's *Celebration* cycle. Time begins to hang heavy as we watch the VIPs still streaming in – the later the arrival, the more important the VIP, I suspect. A violet heart with golden loops of ribbon dangles in front of us. Yes, these pretty baubles have been meaningfully arranged specifically for this farewell: a Playstation for the art-lover's retirement. Certainly spectacular. Meanwhile a fourth speaker has taken the floor. You can't hear a word of it from up here and the guests are growing fidgety. The first of them leave the gallery, fit to drop after standing three-quarters of an hour in the service of pointless erudition. A small, indignant older woman with a sequined dress and a mass of artificial hair takes the arm of a very tall younger man and allows him to escort her outside. "The Germans love to talk, no? " observes Salem. Then Bouman bounds up the stairs. We greet each other, decide to grab a bite somewhere local and abandon the general, winding up at an Italian place in Schöneberg called Bocelli, like the blind tenor. A nice evening of drama – Bocelli, Koons and an arts-world retirement send-off.

22 August
St Petersburg looks like any ordinary city when you drive through it at night; rows of street lights on both sides of the radial highway, a little bit of traffic, a few people out and about, lights on in the houses and restaurants. Looking out of the taxi I see the face of Mireille

Mathieu. Her tear-jerking hits were an accompaniment to my childhood. Is this a journey into the past? Bouman has talked me into attending a conference at the Hermitage. The topic: *The Future of the Universal Museum.*

I get out at the Hotel Europa, its interior courtyard with a glassed-in ceiling and Italianate facade reminiscent of the Mercato shopping mall in Dubai. A harpist by the bar plays something like the soundtrack from *Arielle the Mermaid.* In front of the musician stands an older woman talking at her non-stop, swaying back and forth as if she were trying to mimic the harp's vibrations with her own body movements.

On the Nevsky Prospekt and the Moika embankment, girls passing by on horseback invite you for a night-time ride. Just a ride? In the half-light, they look young and fresh, like high-school teen-agers from the Swiss Jura.

The city is quiet. It draws me through deserted alleyways, past elegant palaces glimmering in the feeble light of the street lamps, and delivers me at the Winter Palace. Apart from the single onion dome rising behind its baroque façade and two discarded transit buses converted into public toilets where vagrants loiter, the entire prospect is one of gigantic, intimidating structures – the architects not content with just emulating Florence, it seems, but intent on outdoing it.

Imported architectural style, showing off in all its absolutist might; a place that, I have to admit, unites beauty and hubris like almost no other. Cartesian order evident in its wide, clam-shaped plaza, in the midst of which stands a column with a sculpture of the Emperor Alexander I, erected to commemorate the victory over Napoleon in the war of 1812. Somewhere behind the high, dull windows, da Vinci's *Madonna Litta* winks through the cocoon of centuries; not far off are the Raphael Loggias, a replica of the loggia in the Vatican City. When St Petersburg was founded three hundred years ago, the tens of thousands of serfs conscripted to build the city were left behind to live in the swamps. The little alley next to the

Winter Palace is called Millionnaya. Visionary brilliance married with an oppressive contempt for human life gave rise to this city. Probably true of all cities in a sense. But almost nowhere else is it so plainly exposed. Who built Babel? Who St Petersburg? Who Dubai? This collection of artifice, imitation, beauty, brutality and delusional grandeur is no oil sheikh's invention. Are we at all aware of how deeply implicated we all are in this inextricable intermingling of idealism and violence, we who burst into tears at the sight of the Piazza San Marco and then fly into a rage at the idea of artificial islands in the Gulf?

Everything old and grand in the Hermitage looks newly built, while the 20th-century embellishments such as the synthetic, ruffled curtains at the windows remain untouched, neglected. The ancient seems young, the recent antiquated. The same might be said of the security guards, all of them women in their sixties and dressed as though off to a ball or the opera. Some of them actually hum to themselves. The Hermitage is their life. And life is only worth living for the arts and their preservation. In this, Soviet-style museum guards have something in common with Nietzsche.

As soon as Bouman and his colleagues have delivered their presentation on how a museum might be modernized without compromising the form and style of its edifice or structure, we are granted an audience with the Director of the Hermitage, Michail Piotrovsky, a short and jovial gentleman with almond-shaped eyes. Apart from the Soviet curtains, his office is how I imagine Prince Nikolai Bolkonsky's library in *War and Peace* to have been, with floor-to-ceiling shelves groaning with weighty tomes, time-worn portraits with softly drawn lines and faded colours, tables and chairs with books and mail stacked upon them – a place where time itself is preserved. Piotrovsky is more approachable than Prince Nikolai, though. We talk about the difficulty of making a fiefdom like the Hermitage attractive to the contemporary without sacrificing itself to it. Bouman marvels at how this museum can be so apparently unperturbed by the fact that, of all the world museums, it has the lowest visitor count in relation to exhibition space. They're happy, Piotrovsky says, not to have to cope with the mass visitor throughput of the Soviet era. What is important is not so much the quantitative aspect as the quality of the experience. From the Western perspective that might be regarded as heresy in terms of business management, I observe wrily. Piotrovsky doesn't disagree. He doesn't have to justify himself – to us or to anyone else. The house he, and his father before him, have directed for decades is possibly the most secure entity in the entire country. Piotrovsky shows photos from the time of the Nazi siege during the Second World War when the Emblem Hall was converted into a field hospital. No one, not even an investment banker, would think of laying a finger on it today.

Later on I take a look at the city's alternatives to Piotrovsky's fiefdom – the Mariinsky Theatre and the Conservatory. Strange how time and again you encounter this insularity in the arts. Architects know nothing of conductors and vice-versa: Bouman's people have never heard of the conductor Mariss Jansons, and there's not a soul in opera who knows who Bouman is.

Banks are taking care of the "structural transformation" on Nevsky, Russia's most famous street, and its environs. Heavy staircases, bought on long-term credit and imported from Turkey or wherever, lead up to the hedge fund headquarters. The deposits are watched over by guards from southern Russia and newly polished caryatids. Magazines with cover shots of Beckham and Mussorgsky are displayed side by side in a kiosk. There's a man there in his fifties with a football for a stomach and bags under his eyes. He must have been an outstanding gymnast in his day, judging by the way he stands on a plank over a moat and sets it wobbling with his knees, all the while screaming into his mobile. He has managed to retain his own national character, the Russian *bisnismen*.

Everywhere this mellow cultural landscape: centuries-old facades, museums and theatres with green and grey coats of paint, worn by age and poverty. They groan under the new age. Capitalism isn't particularly fond of them; otherwise they'd be doing better. Are these factories of the arts that produce only spiritual benefit useful only to despotic regimes?

9

I September

Back in the Gulf. Europa and his mate, now three times his size, are alive and well. At a hotel resort, I happen upon a pond with turtles in it. Or, perhaps I should say, a turtle pool. They're probably on vacation too. Maybe I could build something like it in the apartment, given I never use the second bedroom, or the other rooms much, by dint of constant professional absence. I'll give the idea some thought. Only these beach bums' needs are modest, which is more than can be said for Europa and his heavyweight "trouble-and-strife".

These resorts lend themselves to philosophical reflection on the human zoo. People dawdle along with sun-burned noses and heat-freaked offspring, submitting themselves to engine-powered gondola rides through green, shimmering canals and a landscape of Arab palaces and oases founded in, oh, 2006; they stroll around in souks smelling of popcorn, milk shakes and fresh paint; they puff on their raspberry-flavoured *sheesha* pipes, reclining on Persian ottomans by the pool, as if all of this were somehow real. Returning to this paradise after a vacation in the Harz Mountains, you have to ask yourself what on earth the West has done to make people feel so at ease in this Truman Show; and also what it's done to me, since I too have ended up here.

For the past fourteen days, I've managed to get along without people who are all covered up. Though I'm now able to spot the

Emiratis and Saudis away from home and out of uniform. They're the young couples with deadly serious expressions running the gauntlet of Munich's Maximilianstrasse, anguished by the choice between a coat and skirt from the new autumn collection at Rena Lange or the summer Cherokee Squaw dress by Hermès, this season's choice on the golf courses of the Tegernsee lake; or the large, noisy families in Hyde Park with rollicking adolescents zipping in and out between the roller-bladers while parents and nannies sit in the shade of a maple, waiting stoically for the little monsters to collide catastrophically with one of them.

But now it's back to the dress code of the *dishdash* and *abaya*. Amazing how much money these women spend on something they don't even show. Maybe this is a subtlety peculiar to this culture: distinctiveness beneath the uniformity. Haven't been able to work it out so far. Salem, who is none too fond of putting aside his white gear, confided how embarrassing it is for many overweight Emiratis when they meet each other in the West without their familiar protective covering, not that his lean physique gives him anything to worry about.

8 September

Latifa, Tarek, everyone is talking about Ramadan now it's imminent and how unnecessary it is to do the whole preparation routine – acclimatizing by gradually eating and drinking less each day and waiting until the early afternoon to ingest something, for example. For true celebration, one needs to suffer a little first. Not that they have much choice in the matter. All the same, it is an event. And like any other, Ramadan has its fans.

But there are many too who take pains to ignore it. These non-Muslims remind me a little of the football killjoys during the 2006 World Cup in Germany. They don't want to rain on anyone's parade, but they want no part in it either.

During Ramadan, the day begins with a prayer and breakfast before sunrise, after which there are only prayers and fasting until

dusk. When the sun has disappeared over the Gulf, beyond the artificial islands of The World, and everyone has performed their evening monologue before the Almighty, it's off to the *Iftar* tent (or home) to break the fast. And boy, can they pack it away! I have visited the tent next to the Emirates Tower twice now and it was as you might expect: a monumental buffet with dishes as big as cymbals in the centre, groups of chairs around it where Muslim management (men, for the most part) gorged on kebabs, *shawarma* and beef ribs. This cheerful collective gluttony was accompanied by a Lebanese band, as considerate in the volume of its output as in the frequency of its breaks, which probably meant they didn't miss out on the feasting either.

It is not unknown for a devout Muslim to gain up to three kilos during Ramadan. Catching up on all the food and drink you've had to do without during the day eats into the night, short as it is with the next day starting before sunrise. Despite relaxed working hours during this time, people come to the office ever more exhausted and irritable each day. Now that the holy month has fallen in summer, it's the restriction of drinks and water that really starts to get to people. A quiet depression settles over the city.

Non-believers do indulge their habits at this time, but in restaurants and bistros with curtained windows and screens shielding them from the envious or offended gaze of Muslims. Even Starbucks lower their shutters halfway. This month, only those who can manage to stoop to hip-level will be rewarded with the pleasure of a Grande Frappuccino – luckily for the café chains the average age in Dubai is twenty-four. It has however been known for restaurants to forget about the beginning of Ramadan and carry on with business as usual, which stirred up quite a discussion about this city's Muslim identity.

9 September

According to a report in *The Emirates* newspaper, Mr Matthieu's events company will start broadcasting live opera premieres from the Metropolitan Opera in New York, just four weeks from now. This innovation, they claim, is the first of its kind in the whole of the Middle East to promote opera and classical music. A large influx of music lovers is expected – both tourists and local residents – so the Palladium Theatre, Dubai's largest indoor stage, has been hired for the screenings. The accompanying photo shows Matthieu and Winston, clearly the whizzkid of the team since he would of course have initiated similar projects in Manila, Singapore, Zimbabwe, and maybe even Frankfurt – if the Met hadn't already thought of it last year.

Frau Sturzenegger, with assistance from Latifa and Tarek, has started preparations for the installation of the *Muslim Faces* exhibition. The technicians from Freiburg arrive tomorrow. The translation problems with the catalogue appear to have been resolved.

The Boss's office is pressing us for our opinion on the Museum of the Future yet again. I gave mine before the summer, but that will have been long forgotten by now. I can only assume that Hollywood is asking when they can finally move in with Gore, Einstein and Lincoln, to launch the museum with all proper fanfare.

12 September

The catalogues have arrived, but are being detained at the airport. The Ministry of Information has been called in as a result of various "mistakes" being discovered in the text and images. Latifa is, naturally, pleased with herself. Not out of bloody-mindedness, but because she was right about what wouldn't get through the government censors. You can count on her for that. She is certain the offending phrases were the ones she pointed out during the battle over the translation.

As if by magic, Latifa has an imposing pile of catalogues by her desk. You can't rely on the printers in a situation like this, she opines. She has amended two hundred copies herself. Now she's having them glued. The result is not entirely convincing, but at least we have catalogues for the opening.

13 September

An Emirati looks on during the hanging and installation of *Muslim Faces*. He must be over seventy. His white beard is a little dishevelled and his eyes are glinting red from the sun. After a while he approaches Frau Sturzenegger, who is in the middle of hanging the photo of the impressively adorned Yemeni bride of 1872. He wants to know how much it costs. Frau Sturzenegger gives him an indulgent smile and tells him the photos are part of a collection that is not for sale. The old man sticks to his guns and demands the price of the photo in any case. But he's hitting a brick wall. Nothing can be done. Eventually, he accepts the answer but paces about among the workers hammering away at walls and floor, shaking his head and mumbling to himself in Arabic. He disappears for a while before suddenly materializing to confront Frau Sturzenegger with the question that has been torturing him: *So why are you showing photos if you don't want to sell them?*

15 September
Feverish activity in the US this weekend in a bid to save Lehman Brothers, the global investment bank, from going under.

17 September
The uncensored catalogues are languishing at the printers (who are taking their time with the cost estimates for the pasting) but the opening ceremony can go ahead as planned, thanks to the handiwork of Latifa and her team. Both His Highness Sheikh Majed and The Boss are honouring us briefly with their presence. I extend a welcome to Majed and express my hope that he will be pleased with the exhibition. A little tense, he says he's certain to and, as he turns away, adds: "And if not, I won't be letting on to you." The Boss bleats, amused, in a throaty falsetto. I've never really heard him laugh properly; perhaps he's unable to. A throng has gathered by the entrance, a notable number of Emiratis among them. Word of the Sheikh's arrival has a galvanizing effect and everyone charges eagerly towards him, as if he were about to hand out gift tokens. The German consul-general cleaves his way through the crowd, with little difficulty given his lanky frame, to pay his respects to Majed.

Latifa is wearing a gold-trimmed *abaya* and a scarf the colour the Gulf takes on just after sunset, but she hangs back in the presence of local males. At one point I notice her hobnobbing with Frau Sturzenegger. Perhaps the journey is its own reward when it comes to exchange projects of this kind. If a Swiss museum director and this desert scion of a notable Arab family can conspire in so unabashed a fashion on an occasion so loaded with symbolism, after weeks of communication breakdown, then to hell with what the world's media critics have to say about the mission for culture in the Gulf.

We chose the time between the first and second evening prayer

for the opening, the window between the soul's relief and the loading of the stomach, which also seems to be the propitious hour for whetting the Emirati appetite for art. You can tell just by looking at some of the people here that they haven't been press-ganged into attending but have come of their own volition. Yusuf gives me a surreptitious wave from the hip. He has the air of a teenager, especially beside the hunched man he is linking arms with. That has to be Abdullah. He must have lost fifteen kilos in recent months and appears to have aged by as many years. So delighted am I that they've come that I abandon the Sheikh's clique and hurry over to shake hands. Abdullah can only just raise his head and regards me with difficulty from under his brow. I stay with them as Majed cuts the red ribbon and Frau Sturzenegger utters a few words of greeting. She guides the prince and his courtiers through the exhibition, Yusuf, Abdullah and I tagging along slowly behind them.

At the end, the distinguished gentlemen long gone, I press a bag containing the Arabic catalogue and a series of postcards into Yusuf's hand. He proudly takes out the book, flips through it and tries to get his father interested in it as well. But the old man gazes into the distance and says, in his broken English, that he has seen the pictures of his ancestors just as he would have wished before his end. He has no need of the catalogue because the pictures are now *inside* him. He gestures upwards with his cane, as if he means in heaven rather than in his head.

18 September

For the first time since my arrival here I'm suffused with a feeling I know from my previous professional existence. In the office this morning I luxuriate in the kind of high I've experienced after a successful opera premiere. The volleys of blandishments and excitable chit-chat transcend normal, everyday breeziness: the euphoria is inspired by objective professional results and this has filled everyone with pride. We triumphed, despite the obstacles.

Salem alone seems immune to the enthusiasm. I don't take this amiss but as a sign of his principal rule of behaviour – to remain cool no matter what – until he signals a desire to speak to me alone in my goldfish bowl. At that point I notice he's wearing a red-and-white checked *ghutra* today instead of his usual white one.

My buzz evaporates. The Boss has told him, or directed someone else to tell him (it is increasingly clear that, like me, my young colleague has little direct contact with the people deciding our fate) that the World Museum can be developed further only as a profit-making enterprise. I know it is impossible for him to concur with my view that the decision is absurd, though I suspect he shares it. Nor does he try to contradict me as I paint him a picture of how the German museums will react to this news.

This is not so much about differing opinions on funding models for cultural establishments. It's about something at once much simpler and more complicated: it's about honour and revenge. It arises from *The Principle* – the principle that governs the new rules of the game being written for this city, the unwavering conviction which governs all reasoning in the Emirates Tower and is articulated in all negotiations, decisions and strategies, a conviction which has deep roots in the social and cultural history of these people and their ancestors and their relations with our own ancestors. The Almighty has given them enormous riches, *to show the West what they are capable of*. True, they won't, in Majed's words, be letting on to me. But they will act as this principle dictates, regardless. The most important thing is that the museum makes money, to affirm The Principle, to prove that something that may be unprofitable in the West can be reinvented as profitable here. It is a matter of pride. Anyone who doesn't share that ambition doesn't stand a chance.

Long after Salem has taken his leave, I'm still gasping with helpless rage. The balance sheet for this month is ridiculous: a small, bought-in exhibition at the International Finance Centre. No progress with Khor Dubai. No Theatre Land in Deira, no Pavilion. Countless project proposals and not one of them taken forward. A network of international partnerships in the offing, with no understanding about what these partners are for. I whip a sheet of paper off my desk, sit by the window with a view of the gigantic hole aswarm with thousands of labourers working on the World Trade Centre extension, and jot down the names of all the organizations, artists, agents and architects with whom we have had meaningful contact in recent months. Once finished I write "List of Embarrassments" at the top, and stick it in my jacket pocket. I feel an overmastering urge to add to the list over the coming days.

I dismiss Sheikh Mansour with the same contempt as the Museum of the Future: neither gets to feature on the list. Perhaps the 52nd floor has organized a parallel cultural strategy to include all those projects we have rejected. Could it be that there's a shadow Cultural Council? Happily, I have no time for conspiracy theories. What would be the use? Even were anything to come to pass by that route, it too would be just as ludicrous.

I send a long email to the Germans, filling them in and informing them that top management is currently experiencing difficulties with the World Museum financing model, which will inevitably lead to further long delays.

23 September

Latifa and Mona have locked eyes. I don't know why I'm looking at them. It's the silence, the dead silence that has suddenly descended. The air conditioning has shut itself down. There's more to it than the interruption in the familiar intimacy of the office acoustics. "Take it easy," says Latifa, more to herself than anyone. Tarek turns towards us, mouth agape, the hand holding his mobile phone dropping to his side. Now everyone has noticed. The tower is *rocking*. A slight tremor, and it feels as though we are drifting on gently moving water. And it is the gentleness of this swaying motion that nails me to my chair, as my fingers grow cold and my hands clammy. "Take it easy," Latifa says again, her voice almost cracking. We hear shouts from neighbouring offices. People hurry over. And then there it is again; the discreet swaying motion.

Carmen dials the emergency number listed on our telephones. She's told there is no danger and that the safety regulations stipulate the building is not to be evacuated during earthquakes. There's no time to ponder the logic of this provision because all hell breaks loose when the next shock hits. Everyone grabs their things and joins the crowd rushing down the corridor, looking for the emergency exit. We jostle with fugitives from the upper floors in the stairwell. A manic merriness prevails; jokes and jibes are exchanged, people making an effort to show they're not letting the fear get to them, the ladies teetering precariously on their high heels, some of them carrying briefcases and laptops, whispering into their telephones or cackling amongst themselves. At least no one's panicking. The loneliness of fear is mitigated by collective nervousness, the jostling a godsend in the anxious anticipation of another quake.

Several hundred people have gathered on the piazza in front of the Emirates Towers Boulevard and the crowd is quickly multiplying. Now we are all outdoors in the warm afternoon sunshine, the swelling voices ripple with laughter. There is no announcement or explanation from building management or the onsite security team. People grow restless, more from anxiety about the interruption to their work than from the threat of another shock. A few stalwarts have found a makeshift solution on a park bench where they continue their interrupted meetings. Someone is negotiating with a foreign client on the phone, straining to see his laptop screen in the glare. No one can afford disruptions like this these days, the growing ill-will seems to be saying. The more zealous break away from the throng and return to the Boulevard. Finally someone with a megaphone calls the crowd to order: "The quakes have passed. You may now re-enter the building." We are asked to line up in blocks, floor by floor – a futile suggestion, of course, because everyone is already swarming towards the entrance.

27 September
It takes a few days for the Germans to respond to my email about the World Museum delays. I expect it took them a while to come to terms with the contradiction of this city asking to postpone indefinitely, when it appears time in abundance is the one thing this city totally lacks. The generals tell me they are startled to hear there will be no more progress from our end. Do I need support, from the German Ministry of Foreign Affairs for example? If only they knew. You'd have to explain what the Ministry is first and what it's for. The Berlin Ministry of Foreign Affairs is to the Emirates Tower what a figure skater is to a snow plough.

29 September
The summer has finally drawn to a close and the world's culture salesmen have us on their radar again, bursting to delight us with projects and ideas. A sheikhdom, had I one to give, for a new email address, accessible to no one! Things at the office are going haywire because no one co-ordinates appointments any more. Carmen is working for everyone at once, which is also to say she is working for no one.

I give a cellphone interview to the PR boss of a top Parisian hotel who publishes a monthly bulletin for and about guests, with a serious in-depth discussion piece in each issue. By some oversight, she's managed to catch me this time. I expect she was looking for the spokesman for the exclusive Burj Al Arab hotel. Anyway, we talk about culture in the 21st century, globalization, French Structuralism and Europe's contribution to the modernization of the Middle East, while I'm signalling Carmen not to run away to lunch because I'll be needing her in a minute. But she fails to catch on so it's already too late. The Spanish Ambassador is standing in the door with a delegation of art agents and there's nobody to receive him. Meanwhile the woman on the phone is asking whether I have met the French President's former wife in Dubai. I hurry past the Spanish with a grim nod, as if I were a heating technician called in to see to a burst pipe, give a wordless shrug to the question on the telephone and end the interview in the corridor.

That afternoon in the underground car park I find my car blocked in by three other vehicles. At least the drivers have been kind enough to leave their mobile numbers on the windshields. I call them one after another, becoming increasingly edgy because, among other things, a fellow victim is standing beside me pestering me to call the police. So I'm not exactly on top form when one of the three culprits finally turns up after a further five-minute wait. He's an Indian about my age (with a British passport, as it turns out) who gives me a curt nod and pulls his V8 Lexus SUV out just far enough for me to climb in and creep out of the bay. But the guy's nod has rubbed me up the wrong way, and then I see him emerging from his vehicle with an arrogant expression on his face, checking to ensure I'm not scratching the bilious yellow paintwork of his mobile fortress. I roll down the window and tell him that next time he might care to think twice about where he parks his effing car.

An hour later I get a call from the police. Someone has filed a grievance against me for using the F-word. It seems that our courteous Indian driver squealed and passed on my telephone number. I am naturally contrite but at the same time vexed in the extreme. I tell the officer how it came about and how another offended citizen in the same predicament had advised *me* to press charges against my accuser but I had demurred. The officer is having none of it. I'm to go down to the station.

Instead I call my car park adversary. We exchange a few insults (taking care to eschew the F-word) and then call a draw, agreeing to withdraw our respective threats of police action.

10

12 October

The American museum-chain representative I saw at the *Cityscape* conference in Amman is in to bat again. And me too. This time it's in Hong Kong, at a conference on the future of design, and I have prepared a few thoughts on the subject of whether it is possible to reconfigure traditional arts and crafts without lapsing into kitsch or folklore, a topic of particular relevance to the Gulf region. Dubai's mass importation of the drawings, blueprints, forms, textiles and colours of Western cultures makes it a Babylon of global architecture, fashion, technology and design. They might as well have been imported from the moon for all the cultural relevance they bear to the people expected to consume and live among these things. No trace of the hand of their own creativity, the heritage of their country and its people.

The man from New York evidently sees no reason to rework his Amman presentation for this audience. In slide after slide he conjures up a global empire of culture for the new cosmopolitan elite of capital and ideas, supposedly hungry for all that is contemporary in the arts and its associated merchandising. He has his Hollywood film star helping him out as before, Dennis Hopper on a hot rod through the desert. The motorcycle brand gets its due mention this time since the conference owes its existence to their sponsorship.

Later, I go for a drink in the hotel lobby. A Pritzker architecture prizewinner briefs his lackeys on where he wants his five aluminium suitcases delivered. It will be the umpteenth architect's model of the extreme fantastical I've seen today and I'm as good as certain that none of them will ever be built, given world markets are in meltdown and on the verge of collapse. I'd hazard a guess that design for the 21st century will take a completely different turn from the architecture of excess we've now come to expect. But the jury is still out and it's reassuring to know it has ninety-one years ahead of it to review the evidence.

The New Yorker takes a seat next to me and is actually showing signs of exhaustion. Like a commanding officer demanding the utmost from his frontline troops, he is completely obsessed and fretting about his new franchises in Baku, Astana, Vilnius, Athens and Istanbul. Threats of civil disturbances and teetering governments are giving him cause for concern. Singapore went off well, but there are no other promising signs in the Far East. A similar mindset to the Pentagon's, perhaps.

13 October

I wake early, with yesterday's presentations drifting through my mind. With the exception of a Japanese and a Chinese from San Francisco, all the speakers were Westerners. Even the man charged with representing the Gulf is from the West. We can hardly be surprised at the ambivalence of Asians and Arabs. Of course they want our glass beads, but they know they're glass beads. They even know that glass beads are all we have left. No more silver bullets, only perishable goods, even if we do try to pass them off as sustainable. So contagious is our arrogance that it teaches the very people who have gone through our schools and decided to take their chances on other continents to despise us and overestimate themselves. Whatever it takes to bind them more tightly to us and render them even more dependent. No, the thing going on here in the East is not yet the beginning of something entirely new. That chance may never come again. Every idea is reduced to bathos, every manoeuvre trapped in the sticky embrace of economic inter-dependence. The New World will not emancipate itself from the Old, it will drag the Old behind it like a bride's train, it will wrap itself up in it until you can no longer make out the New. There will be no autonomy, either for them or for us.

28 October

First rain. The announcement comes in a phone call to Salem from his mother in the neighbouring emirate of Sharjah. She tells him to look out of the window before it's too late. Rain is a blessing, a blessing that lasts just a few minutes. Salem's mother is right to make the call.

II

1 November

His Highness, the ruler of Dubai, has called on the people for wisdom and patience as the country confronts the economic crisis, according to *The Emirates*. The question is, wisdom and patience from whom? Does he mean Abdul-Hamid, who sits quietly in his Sailing House hoping he will not be prosecuted in a court of law, and waiting for a storage solution for Hassan's new paintings? Or the boss of Arab Properties, who just last week unveiled a new project to build the world's tallest tower at a thousand metres high? Or perhaps he means the Azerbaijani home owner who purchased a Palm Island estate for 4.5 million US dollars three months ago and can't get rid of it for two million now, even after throwing two of his Bentleys into the deal? Or is His Highness referring to the construction worker from Kerala who showed me a Polaroid of his father a few months ago?

Al Adheem has announced a third of its work force will be made redundant "for operational reasons". Employees are summoned to the personnel office and sent away with a letter of cancellation and immediate paid holiday of varying duration (depending on rank). They are given two hours to clear their desks and hand over important business documents including health insurance cards. We receive mass emails from co-workers saying their farewells. Azad is among them: Dear Friends, This is my last day at Al Adheem, from now on I can be contacted at the following address in Norway …

4 November

A Dutch woman has been found stabbed in a shopping mall car park. The murder victim was the wife of a well-known banker and was apparently wearing too much jewellery. Up until now, this well-lit country has been promoted as a virtually crime-free zone. From the newspaper's description, you would think the story was about the murder of a prostitute.

5 November

Rumours are self-fulfilling. Property prices have fallen by a quarter in the past six weeks; developers have billions in accrued liabilities with no idea how to cover them. The Theatre Land plot has been sold to Sheikh Mansour for development as a large-scale car park for luxury vehicles. I recall meeting a theatre troupe in Kentucky in the early nineties whose stage was part of a car park and whose productions were kept afloat by the parking fees. Maybe the financing of culture will work out after all. On the other hand, six unidentified Porsche Cayennes were found abandoned on the Emirates Towers parking deck last week. They're going up for auction. Question is, who's going to pay the parking fees.

In the office, an air of anxious under-employment prevails. The outlook for existing projects is uncertain. We have received no instructions or information but are cautious with production scheduling. Service without guaranteed funding, one might say, or at least any guarantee that it will continue much longer. New proposals are turned away. Salem appears to know more than he is allowed to say, and seems tired and insecure. Nevertheless, he volunteers the opinion that the Cultural Council is an important governmental organization and will carry on as planned.

11 November

Andras, a senior man in the government treasury, reports over lunch in an Emirates Towers fast food joint that the money will last approximately eight weeks more. The city's credibility is so low that loans are now attracting interest rates of 20 percent. Several government agencies have been merged, and a new treasury boss has been appointed who comes from Singapore and flies home to his wife every Thursday. The new man has hired four young Frenchmen with a reputation for having the best contacts in the international investment business. The young men speak almost no English and blithely converse in their native tongue, assuming that they will be understood by no one. Andras understands them though and is now following their conversation as they pick the place to pieces, having a good deal of fun in the process. None of them, Andras says, believes they will be staying in the post for more than four weeks. Until then, it's all about pulling in the cash.

14 November

They turned up at the deserted atrium at the International Finance Centre boulevard late yesterday evening. Six clueless Pakistani handymen armed with a single screwdriver and four hammers. Right in front of the desolated Frau Sturzenegger, they smashed the entire exhibition structure to pieces. She had returned for sentimental reasons after her staff had removed the photos from the walls and taken them to safety. It must have been a while since the workmen had seen a woman come apart at the seams, and once they noticed the emotional impact they were having on the poor curator they took a special delight in ripping the walls apart. She was involuntary witness to a commando raid.

When she finally called me, protesting bitterly, and passed me over to speak to the foreman, it turned out he spoke practically no English. I arrived forty-five minutes later, but the deed had already been done. The splintered walls lay stacked like firewood by the sliding doors, about to be loaded onto a truck.

Neither Latifa nor Salem can tell me who gave the order for this senseless destruction. Our first venue, and probably our only one for a very long time. Until yesterday, I had assumed we would be able to keep the foyer space and use it for subsequent exhibitions. The plan was to rent it out commercially when we ourselves had no use for it. Somebody has clearly decided otherwise and, from the way my Emirati colleagues are evading my questions, I can tell they know who is behind it.

Four thousand visitors, three hundred and eleven catalogues sold and a few hundred posters and postcards taken off our hands. The exhibition walls are on their way to the dump, while fifteen hundred catalogues still await approval. The VIP packs with material on the exhibition have still not been sent, though Latifa has been telling me for weeks how she is organizing the distribution. Some consolation at least: a private collector has expressed interest in showing the exhibition in Kuwait City.

22 November

Abandoned cars, apartments, buildings, boats, evacuated offices and silent accounts: these days, the siren song of capitalism might be playing everywhere on the globe but nowhere is it more raw, honest and radical than here. The city has gorged itself on whatever it could gulp down. Now it's spitting it all back out: businesses, materials, people. The sun sinks into the Gulf at around five-thirty, and there on the horizon are the silhouettes of freighters, multiplying by the day. They're transporting steel, glass, lifts and ceramic tiles, waiting to be disembarked at the docks of a city that had planned to build over a four-million-square-metre plan, using twenty-five percent of the world's cranes. Planes have been chartered to take redundant labourers out of the country. The men line up in their camps and are told to leave their work clothing and helmets in a pile before they are driven to an airfield near the desert. It has to be done quickly because many of the men, in expectation of three years' steady income, are in debt to their neighbours at home who have put up the money to enable them to get jobs here in the first place. Now they can't return to their villages. Many see suicide as the only option. And people in this country don't want that on their hands.

Emails pour in warning against panic selling and using credit cards, and also ones warning about those self-same warnings. A young Russian bursts into tears in the Emirates Towers lift. She has been renting apartments and houses on commission and has not earned a dirham in weeks. And then Danny writes, a fifty-year-old American I met at a party at the Fairmont Hotel. He was, until yesterday, a software buyer for a Taiwanese computer company. Now he's stranded on a business trip in Riga because not only has the company fired him, they've cancelled his phone and credit cards. His visa is still valid for a week. "The wolves howl at the door," writes Danny. "Need a gardener?"

23 November

Just as I had almost forgotten about him, Winston shows up again, looking for Salem. He's brought important news, which of course cannot be entrusted to me, from the opening of the Museum of Islamic Art in Doha. All the same, I seem to be worthy of a report on the opening ceremony. Not surprisingly, Winston had been seated right next to Robert de Niro, Ronnie Wood and Damien Hirst, with a good view of the Arabian Highnesses rubbing noses on the red carpet before their tour of the Pei building. Winston is thrilled, naturally – with the ceremony and, as far as he is able to describe it, the museum itself.

Inquiries at the Palladium by *The Emirates* have revealed that the live opera broadcasts from the New York Met have been stopped after only three performances. The report prompts a French opera lover to call me, because she knows exactly why: even at the inaugural screening there was neither introduction nor programme and seats in the front rows reserved for VIPs remained empty. The following two broadcasts started at 11 p.m. and the auditorium was chilled to 18°C, as if in expectation of a rave. And then there was a premiere by an American composer and a production of *Salome*, with the "Dance of the Seven Veils" heavily cut to avoid upsetting the sensibilities of Muslim visitors. They needn't have worried. Those tender souls were absent from all three performances. My informant also tells me that Matthieu's office has gone into liquidation, or so she's heard.

When I ask Salem about it, he says Matthieu's people are in the process of restructuring. So, why the insecurity on his part? Then he confides that he has postponed his wedding. Not because of his 45-Day Syndrome or its fall-out. It's just not the right time.

26 November
Reports are flying around that Marwan, the President of Al Adheem, has been placed under house arrest.

27 November
Bouman and Abdul-Hamid have found a solution to the lack of space at the Sailing House: The Shelter, a temporary pavilion on the beach not far from a sailing club. They can stay there until early next year as long as the Sheikh (to whom the land belongs) does not change his mind.

I know from Bouman that all the projects he was contracted for in the region have been suspended. The building of his own office in the city and the three years of preparatory work are all for the birds, at least for the time being. I suspect his contracts in the Far East and America are faring no better. But after just two working days with the people at the Sailing House there's now something resembling a lighthouse with a party tent attached on the dunes of Umm Suqeim.

With white stubble now illuminating his ruddy, narrow face, Bouman looks a bit like a pilot. Only the cap and uniform are

missing. He leads me to his latest masterpiece, Abdul-Hamid and Hassan staying close by his side. From the east The Shelter looks something like a turtle, inquisitively stretching its head skywards. I know the pose from my own two creatures when I show up at the turtle tank with food. The towering section of the annex and the tent walls are pieced together from the discarded planks of old fishing dhows. The pavilion gleams deep brown against the sea, as if preparing for takeoff. The circular floor of about twelve metres in diameter houses an assortment of Hassan's installations on the subject of the sea.

Hassan looks a little confused today. His hair is sticking up on one side like a visor and his eyes behind his glasses look like those of a giant fish in an aquarium. He takes me by the arm and shows me the works on display: stained hawser, looped around stones, as used in dyke construction; flip-flops and synthetic flotsam ensnared in nets; a few oil paintings with expressive and naïve views of surf. Bouman waves me over to look at the tower section. It's five metres high and tapers to a cone at the top (with a small opening at the apex) and has roughly the same layout as the pavilion. There are no artworks here but a few rows of chairs in front of a stage designed for theatre and music. Last night's inaugural event was provided by a group of Somalis and their drums. Bouman says it has good acoustics.

You can see The Shelter from a distance because there is no other building so close to the beach. It draws a lot of people; tourists and residents, the puzzled and the curious, not quite sure what to make of it. Abdul-Hamid has persuaded a beverage salesman to set up his stand just next door and visitors, after seeing the exhibition, do actually sit down in front of the pavilion with a bottle of grapefruit juice or mineral water, attracting more and more of a crowd.

So, things have actually worked out for the first non-commercial public art space in the city. And without the help of a Cultural Council. Three hundred square metres of freedom on the beach. Until further notice. Police and coastguard drive past at a stately pace in their chunky four-by-fours and wave at Abdul-Hamid from the open windows.

28 November

Abdullah is dying. It all started when he caught a chill, outdoors in the wadi near Hatta. Yusuf says he now looks like the old man in our catalogue, a Bedouin with a long white beard, a mass of brown wrinkles, and eyes wide open, as a result of the magnesium flash of the camera, perhaps. The man props himself up on a cane with considerable effort, standing with his back to the wall of a house. His eyes are so brightly illuminated you see just the shadows of the irises. You can look through them to another world.

30 November

The big turtle has disappeared. Mary Jane, who cleans here twice a week and takes care of the animals in my absence, still has tears in her eyes and says she turned the apartment upside-down this morning without finding our fatso. Europa is sitting alone on the artificial island, sadly stretching his mouth in the air as though calling for his monstrous bride. Mary Jane assures me that she has neither removed the animal from the water, nor did she discover any trace of it around the aquarium. I try to dismiss the thought of her feeding it to one of the tiger sharks in Dubai Mall. A good pound of live turtle could not have vanished into thin air, of course, but hours of searching and inquiries with my neighbour Khalil yield nothing but unhelpful speculation. I try to accept the fact that our female will remain disappeared. Evidently such a demise can be ascribed to unnatural as well as natural causes.

12

2 December

A national holiday. The country has turned thirty-seven. I was among the last to leave the office last night, shortly before eight, when an American designer responsible for the Emirates Towers interior design appeared in the doorway with a stack of tee shirts on her arm and laid one of them on my desk. It bore the slogan "I love the UAE". I have received an XXL, presumably befitting my rank. I could probably pull it on over an astronaut's suit.

The fireworks have been curtailed this year, Salem had warned me. Come to think of it, I remember seeing them late this evening and realize now I have noticed almost none of the usual associated activity. No rowdy Emirati offspring, drunk on enthusiasm, spraying themselves and their cars with the national colours and driving at least one car to the junkyard to set it ablaze on a giant bonfire. Even the public parade, which has consumed Salem and the team in preparations over the past few days, almost sneaks along the pavement without the rest of the city noticing.

3 December

Eid al-Adha – the big religious holiday, directly after the national day celebrations. For us that means a week's vacation. So I'm alone in the office. The tower and the city are almost deserted, because the pagans are all catching 500-euro flights to Katmandu or the Maldives or jetting off to Venice, while there's still money in the bank. And the believers are all doing obeisance to the All-Powerful. Apart from a few tourist taxis and Indian workers in Toyota flatbed trucks, there's little other traffic on Sheikh Zayed Road. The cranes are at a standstill.

10 December

Salem implores me for leniency for his Emirati colleagues and himself. The ruler told some of those closest to him a few days ago: "For many years you have run the straight race. The time has come for a well-deserved break."

As a member of quite another kind of athletics club, I am compelled every day at least to complete the distance to my desk, to sort my overflowing inbox into one-way emails (no answer) and two-way emails (guarded answer). The ruler's analogy of the runners and their break appeals to me. So the Bedouin roots are there after all. The caravan has travelled steadfastly through the desert of modernization, trading all its goods with the 21st century, and now it's turning back to the oasis to sit out the sandstorm of economic crisis, putting its faith in the Almighty ordaining better times to come.

12 December

My Lord, make this a City of Peace, and feed its people with fruits
– such of them as believe in Allah and the Last Day.
The Holy Qur'an, Surah 2: 126

And what is to become of everyone else? The city is still not back in business. The hush of the holidays has given way to an involuntary paralysis that has also come over me in the course of the past week. The atmosphere is best evoked by Erik Satie's *Caresse*, which I've loaded on my laptop to hum along to. In the office twilight hours, it feels as though I've missed the last plane out or have been forgotten in an evacuation. I want them back – the swinging cranes, the rattling compressors, the traffic jams and the assaults on the shopping malls. Hello, anyone there? This calm is getting to me. More stress, please!

Finally Latifa, Mona and Tarek decide to show their faces. All seem exhausted, as if they have just survived an expedition through the mountains of Musandam. It's probably just the hangover from chilling out at the family oasis. Carmen isn't expected back until next week. She's visiting her family in Mumbai.

Public sector operations are being restructured. Al Adheem is dissolved. Someone quietly cleared out the offices over the holiday. Marwan is reportedly still under arrest. And what has become of Mohammed, the young schoolmaster-type whose brash telephone conversation a year ago started it all for me? His fate will doubtless remain a mystery because contact with the 52nd floor appears to have been broken off. Salem gives the impression of not having received any instructions and doesn't seem to know much more than the rest of us. So basically we're acting out a pointless mime.

13 December

The one-and-a-half-billion-dollar Atlantis super-hotel, whose opening fourteen days ago cost the organizers twenty million dollars and which was so brilliantly lit it could be seen from outer space, is making the headlines again. The international media have already reported on Robert de Niro and Charlize Theron at the opening and the German media on Boris Becker's reunion there with his formerly adored beloved; now comes news that the South African proprietor has every reason to pray. The rate of occupancy is so miserable that rooms can now be had at the rock-bottom price of thirty euros a night. It's now a serious alternative to a one-room apartment in Bur Dubai or Deira for many Indian and Filipino low-earners.

15 December

Year-end party at the agreeably unostentatious consul-general's house. Among the guests is a camel vet who relocated here from Wiesbaden twenty-five years ago. The man, though he's elegantly dressed and probably younger, reminds me of the European dropouts I met in the forest villages of Kerala – people with white hair living under roofs made of palm and tulip tree who, having reached their seventies, were preparing for transfiguration. The camel vet doesn't hold the comparison against me and divulges that he has already given some thought about what should be done with his mortal shell – because he doesn't want to go back to Germany, not even dead. But there are no cemeteries for non-believers in this city.

He's heard of people hastily converting their dead to Hinduism. Even the wood for cremation has to be imported. But there are quite a few Westerners here who came decades ago and are now inching towards the end. Rumour has it there's a Brit planning to open an undertaker's. The man leased a plot of land some time ago and has already had it consecrated by a priest in Jebel Ali. It's a business that probably has better prospects than the property sector.

20 December

Paralysis gives way to pre-Christmas fever. At home, or what once was home, *Hansel and Gretel* is back on the opera playbill. Our middle-school children clamour in the foyer under the yellow light of the crystal chandeliers trailing exasperated teachers behind them, as the buzzer left over from GDR days signals the end of the advertisement-free intermission and the start of the showdown at the witch's little house.

I won't be going; won't be travelling to the capital at all but via Hanover to Clausthal and to the mountains.

At the office, my colleagues give me a wink and a firm handshake. Latifa even ventures an unseemly hug. Carmen's face betrays anxiety and I ask whether everything is okay. And now the others are speaking among themselves she finds the courage to answer in lowered tones that she's worried about her future. "When the government starts announcing layoffs, then the Indians will be the first to go," she frets. How is she supposed to make ends meet and help her family in Mumbai? My conciliatory response comes across as vapid and feeble. We both know there is nothing we can do.

Salem escorts me to the lift. I tell him this feels a bit like a final farewell, even though I'll be coming back. "I know," he says, leaving it open as to whether he refers to my farewell or return. "We're going to be offered the Al Adheem offices, supposedly," he adds, as if trying to persuade me to stay. "So you think we could afford their 37th-floor offices?" I ask. Salem shrugs. "Maybe next year," he says, with a crooked grin.

31 December

Europa's doing well. Carmen has been attending to him in my absence. People are dying in Gaza. New Year celebrations have been cancelled in Dubai, no firework displays permitted. The new director of my former opera house wants to put *Israel in Egypt* back on the programme and asks whether I can come to Berlin for a discussion on Palestine and the Middle East.